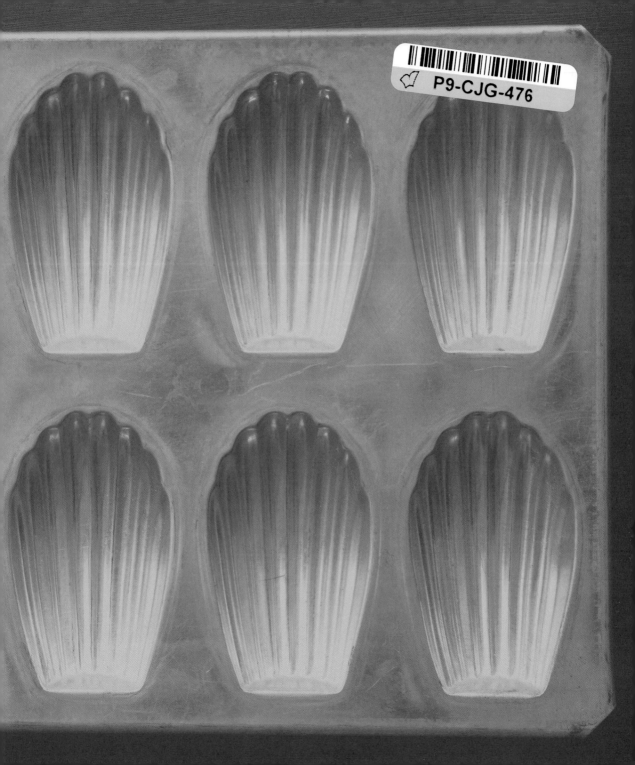

we love madeleines

WE LOVE
madeleines

BY **MISS MADELEINE**

PHOTOGRAPHS BY **ANTONIS ACHILLEOS**

CHRONICLE BOOKS

SAN FRANCISCO

I love madeleines. But, more important, *we* love madeleines, and this book would not exist without the madeleine lovers—and bakers—around the world. First and foremost, thank you to all the recipe developers who shared their special creations for this book. Your enthusiasm for madeleines fueled this work, while your unexpected flavor combinations and lovingly crafted recipes will surely inspire countless bakers, as they did me. I must also offer an enormous *merci* to my brilliant editors, Amy Treadwell and Kate Willsky, who formed this collection of recipes into a simply scrumptious book, just as a madeleine pan molds a bowl of batter into a beautiful cookie! Thank you, too, to my beloved *grand-mère* Yolaine and her dear friend Marcel, who would have eaten this book up; to Madame Dubois, who generously offered her flour sacks as my childhood bed; and to the talented team at Chronicle Books—Vanessa Dina, Tera Kilip, Doug Ogan, Claire Fletcher, Peter Perez, and David Hawk—who always went above and beyond the call of duty and never shirked any opportunities to taste-test. Now let's bake!

—M.M.

Library of Congress Cataloging-in-Publication Data available.
ISBN 978-1-4521-0290-0

Manufactured in China

Designed by vanessa dina
Photo background patterns by repot depot
Prop styling by spork
Food styling by cristina besher
Typesetting by dc typography

10 9 8 7 6 5 4 3 2

Chronicle Books LLC
680 Second Street
San Francisco, California 94107
www.chroniclebooks.com

BON APPÉTIT!

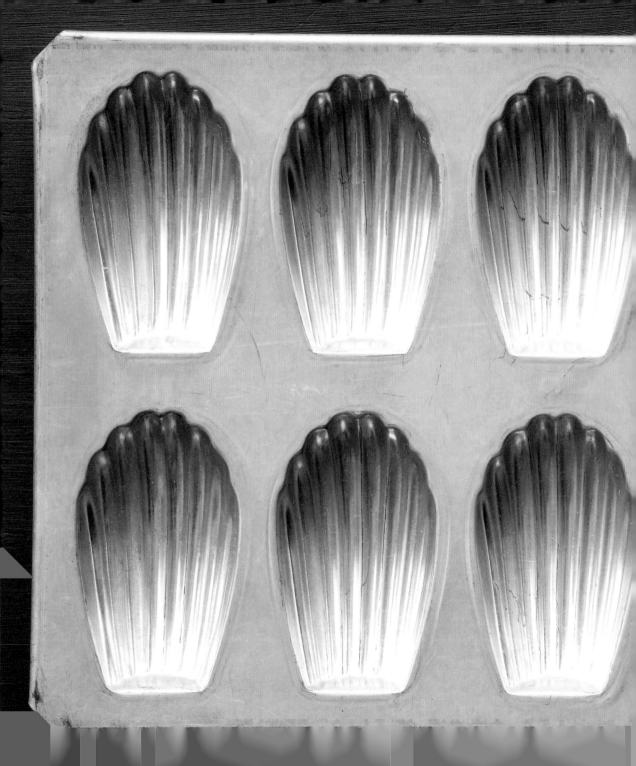

CONTENTS

Don't be deceived by the madeleine's small size; each is a whole world of flavor bearing scores of stories, told and untold. This petite book, too, holds far more than meets the eye. Besides containing the recipes and stories of dozens of different bakers—more on that in a moment—it has been almost 150 years in the making, the first glimmer of its existence sparkling through in the mid-1800s. You see, my great-grandmother Mamie, who lived in a small village in northern France and was Marcel Proust's math tutor, happened to

witness her young charge's first bite of madeleine. Teacher and student kept in touch, and many years later, when Proust had become a successful author, he wrote Mamie a letter describing the now-famous "madeleine episode," in which one bite of madeleine transported him back to that late afternoon in Illiers.

After some decades, when I was about the age Marcel had been, Mamie gave me a classic madeleine and explained how a student of hers had once been "transported" by the little cake. Not yet grasping the subtleties of figurative language, I was enthralled: Where would the madeleine take *me*? Rennes? Berlin? New York City? Neptune? Quickly disillusioned (I opened my eyes and was still standing on the cobbled café sidewalk), I understood that Marcel and Mamie had meant to suggest a journey in one's mind to a lovely and distant place, foreign or familiar, that touches often dormant parts of one's being.

Now that was all well and good, but I wasn't sold. I wanted to go places, real places. And I was convinced that madeleines were my golden ticket.

Turns out I was right.

My love for all things in a pastry case continued to flourish (influenced in no small part by growing up above the kitchen of a Parisian pâtisserie), and by the time I'd turned five and began to bake on my own, I had focused my attention on madeleines. My childhood and adolescence were shrouded in a flurry of flour and scented with the comforting warmth of preheating ovens. As soon as I'd saved enough francs, I set out to explore the globe's vast pantry, seeking new flavors and culinary techniques that would make my madeleines delicious and exciting, each batch different from the last.

Now, years later, madeleines continue to pull me in all directions; there are always new variations and novel flavors that make each little cake a singular experience, always new cities to visit, and new people and places from which to draw inspiration. And nothing speaks to this untapped abundance more than the vibrant community of one-of-a-kind madeleine bakers around the world. This book is a celebration of their work and a testament to the undefinable and ever-evolving essence of the madeleine.

We have the Internet to thank for the delectable diversity within these pages. I knew I wanted to gather my recipes from the field and came up with the idea of crowdsourcing the material—an idea that the fine folks at Chronicle Books loved! Through a blog post and some savvy social-media navigation, I put out a call for home bakers to share their beloved madeleine recipes with us, and the passionate responses came pouring in! From matcha to maple pecan to molasses spice, flavors flooded the in-box, coming from as far away as Italy and Spain as well as right from Chronicle's own backyard of San Francisco. Recipes arrived from journalists and farmers, illustrators and digital media gurus, even one from a full-time madeleine peddler who prowls the streets of San Francisco dispensing her treats while dressed up as Raphael, her favorite Teenage Mutant Ninja Turtle. Every madeleine is uniquely yummy, and you'll inevitably add your own story to the ingredient list, mixing your own flair right into the batter.

Because these recipes come from so many different sources, you'll see all sorts of different techniques for crafting the perfect madeleine, from chilling batter to rotating baking trays to sifting your flour *just so*. They are all in here, so you can see the wide range of tricks and tips bakers use and find the perfect solution for you—unless, of course, you come up with your own strategy! Let your imagination play, and let the vibrant and quirky people behind these recipes inspire your baking. Each recipe can be followed to a tee, guaranteeing a lip-smacking result, or you can look at these pages as canvases to color with your own favorite tastes. Make new memories with each batch, and try your best to remember them, because it won't be long before they're gobbled up, and memories—plus some crumbs and a sweet-smelling kitchen—will be all that's left.

ALL ABOUT MADELEINE PANS AND OTHER HELPFUL TOOLS

Madeleines are truly a simple cookie. They are perfect paired with any morning drink or dessert dip or just left on their own. They require very little time to prepare and only a few pieces of bakeware. Here are some tools that will make your baking experience easier; but, really, it's all about the madeleine pan!

Stand mixer

Don't worry if you don't have a stand mixer; although it is easier to work with, a handheld mixer gets the job done, too! Mixing by hand is not recommended; the eggs and sugar need vigorous mixing to get the appropriate volume needed for perfect madeleines.

Sifter

You'll use this to make sure your delicate batters are free of lumps and silky smooth.

Madeleine pan

There are three different types of madeleine pans: SILICONE, NONSTICK, and SHINY METAL. There are disputes over which is the best.

A SILICONE madeleine pan is flexible and makes it easier to remove your treats from the pan. They come in gorgeous bright colors and are the perfect bakeware for the modern baker.

A metal NONSTICK madeleine pan is probably the easiest to find and cook with, but the cookies will brown faster.

If you want to bake like a French *pâtissier*, then go for the SHINY METAL pan. Make sure you give more attention to buttering and flouring the tins so the madeleines don't stick.

All three types of madeleine pans come in two sizes: Regular madeleine pans make twelve madeleines; mini-madeleine pans usually make twenty-four cookies, though you can sometimes find mini pans that make eighteen cookies. Since many of the recipes in this book make twenty-four madeleines, I own two pans, so I don't need to re-grease.

MADELEINE SIZES

Unless otherwise indicated, the recipe yields are based on a regular-size madeleine pan. Mini-madeleine pans generally make twice as many cookies.

A NOTE ABOUT THE RECIPE METHODS

The recipes in this book have been developed by a variety of creative bakers, and you'll find that the directions vary from recipe to recipe. Guess that proves that there's more than one way to bake a madeleine.

CHILLING THE PANS

Some folks swear that the hump on their madeleine is higher if they chill the pans before filling the molds with batter. I have tried it both ways and have not seen a significant difference in the final madeleine.

REFRIGERATING THE BATTER

This is another method that some of the recipes use to get a higher hump. Again, I have not found a significant difference when using refrigerated batter versus room-temperature batter.

GREASING THE PANS

Always generously grease a madeleine pan, whether you have a nonstick pan or not. After each batch has baked and you've removed the madeleines, let the pan cool, and be sure to re-grease the pan before baking another batch.

PIPING BATTER

Use a pastry bag or a plastic zip-top bag with a corner snipped off to pipe the batter into the pans.

REMOVING MADELEINES FROM THE PAN

Admittedly, madeleines can sometimes be a bit difficult to remove from the pans after baking. Some people think they need to be turned out onto a wire rack immediately after they are removed from the oven, and others think it's best to let them cool in the pan for a few minutes first. Generous buttering seems to help, but you'll likely get the best results by following the individual recipe instructions. When I bake them, if they don't immediately come out of the pans after baking, I let them cool for about 5 minutes and try it again. If they still aren't releasing from the pan, I use a spoon or blunt knife to gently remove them.

DRIZZLING AND GLAZING

Little plastic squeeze bottles are great for drizzling chocolate and other glazes over the madeleines.

STORING

You can store madeleines for about three days in a tightly covered container at room temperature, but they are at their best when enjoyed the same day they are baked, either warm or at room temperature.

CLASSIC MADELEINES

the basic
madeleine

1 CUP/115 G ALL-PURPOSE FLOUR, PLUS MORE FOR DUSTING THE PAN

1/4 TSP BAKING POWDER

1/8 TSP SALT

3 EGGS, AT ROOM TEMPERATURE

1 EGG YOLK, AT ROOM TEMPERATURE

1/3 CUP/65 G GRANULATED SUGAR

3/4 TSP VANILLA EXTRACT

6 TBSP/85 G UNSALTED BUTTER, MELTED AND COOLED TO ROOM TEMPERATURE, PLUS MORE FOR GREASING THE PAN

POWDERED SUGAR FOR DUSTING

NAME: *Agnes Devereux*

LOCATION: *New Paltz, NY*

MAD MORSEL: *Though she had lived in Paris for two years, Agnes first encountered (and fell in love with) madeleines at a pâtisserie in Manhattan. Years later, when she was wrangling with the planning board for approval of the restaurant she wanted to open, she brought a fresh-baked batch of her homemade madeleines to the meeting and got her permit that very night. She is now the proud owner of the Village Tea Room where she makes madeleines in addition to many other delightful baked goods.*

Into a small bowl, sift together the flour, baking powder, and salt and set aside.

In the bowl of a stand mixer fitted with the paddle attachment, beat together the eggs, egg yolk, granulated sugar, and vanilla until the batter is thick enough to fall from the beater in a slow "ribbon." Sprinkle the flour mixture over the egg mixture. Using a rubber spatula, carefully fold in the flour mixture until just combined.

In a small bowl, whisk one-third of the batter into the melted butter, then fold the butter mixture into the remaining batter until just combined. Let the batter rest for at least 1 hour.

Position a rack in the center of the oven and preheat to 350°F/180°C/gas 4. Grease a madeleine pan with melted butter and dust with flour, tapping out any excess.

Spoon or pipe the batter into the prepared pan, filling each mold three-quarters full. Bake until the madeleines are golden brown around the edges, 8 to 10 minutes.

Immediately turn out the madeleines onto a wire rack and let cool. Dust with powdered sugar and serve.

the basic
with vanilla bean

1⅓ CUPS/170 G PASTRY FLOUR, PLUS MORE FOR DUSTING THE PANS

1 TSP BAKING POWDER

½ TSP SALT

3 EGGS, AT ROOM TEMPERATURE

⅔ CUP/130 G SUGAR

1 TBSP HONEY

½ CUP/115 G UNSALTED BUTTER, MELTED AND COOLED TO ROOM TEMPERATURE, PLUS MORE FOR GREASING THE PANS

1 VANILLA BEAN, SPLIT LENGTHWISE AND SEEDS SCRAPED FROM THE POD (RESERVE THE POD FOR ANOTHER USE; SEE NOTE)

MAKES 48 MADELEINES

NAME: *Serena Giacometti*
LOCATION: *Santa Maria di Sala, Venice, Italy*
MAD MORSEL: *Though she loves cooking traditional Italian cuisine, Serena's sweet tooth led her to this classic French treat. Adapted from a recipe by the great French pastry chef Gaston Lenôtre, this one is as authentic as they come.*

Into a medium bowl, sift together the pastry flour, baking powder, and salt and set aside.

In the bowl of a stand mixer fitted with the paddle attachment, beat the eggs, sugar, and honey on medium-high speed until light and fluffy and doubled in volume, about 5 minutes. Using a rubber spatula, fold the flour mixture into the egg mixture until just combined. Add the melted butter and vanilla seeds and mix until combined. Refrigerate the batter for at least 2 hours or up to 24 hours.

Position one rack in the upper quarter of the oven and another in the center and preheat to 450°F/230°C/gas 8. Generously grease two madeleine pans with melted butter and dust them with flour, tapping out any excess.

Spoon or pipe the batter into the prepared pans, filling each mold no more than three-quarters full. Reduce the oven temperature to 400°F/200°C/gas 6 and bake, staggering the pans so that the top pan is not directly over the lower one until the center of the madeleines starts to form a depression, 3 to 5 minutes. Reduce the oven temperature again, this time to 350°F/180°C/gas 4, rotate the pans from front to back and upper to lower, and continue baking until the depression becomes a little hump (characteristic of all good madeleines) and the edges just start to color, about 4 minutes more.

Immediately turn out the madeleines onto a wire rack and let cool. Wipe out the pans and let cool. Re-grease and re-flour the pans, re-fill with batter, and continue baking until all the batter has been used. Serve warm or at room temperature.

NOTE:

The leftover vanilla pod can be used to make vanilla sugar, which can be used in any recipe calling for sugar. Into a tall mason jar, pour about ½ cup/100 g granulated sugar. Push the vanilla pod into the sugar so that the pod is sticking straight up. Fill the rest of the jar with more sugar and close with a tight-fitting lid. Let sit at room temperature for at least 2 weeks before using. It keeps for at least 2 months.

the basic
with lemon zest

¾ CUP/170 G UNSALTED BUTTER, PLUS 2 TBSP FOR GREASING THE PANS

¾ CUP/90 G ALL-PURPOSE FLOUR, PLUS MORE FOR DUSTING THE PANS

4 EGGS, AT ROOM TEMPERATURE

PINCH OF FINE-GRAIN SEA SALT

2/3 CUP/130 G GRANULATED SUGAR

ZEST OF 1 LARGE LEMON

1 TSP VANILLA EXTRACT

POWDERED SUGAR FOR DUSTING

MAKES 24 MADELEINES

NAME: *Souris Hong-Porretta*
LOCATION: *Los Angeles*
MAD MORSEL: *Souris started baking madeleines to give her French husband a taste of home. She's become such an expert that she can whip out several dozen in less than an hour, and she has sent them to friends all over the world, from Italy to Afghanistan.*

In a small heavy pan, melt the ¾ cup/170 g butter over medium heat and continue heating until it turns brown and releases a delicious nutty aroma, about 20 minutes. Using a fine-mesh strainer lined with a paper towel, strain the solids from the butter into a small bowl. Discard the solids. Set aside and let cool to room temperature.

Position one rack in the upper quarter of the oven and another in the center and preheat to 350°F/180°C/gas 4. Generously grease two madeleine pans with the remaining 2 tbsp butter and dust them with flour, tapping out any excess.

In the bowl of a stand mixer fitted with the whisk attachment, whisk together the eggs and salt on medium-high speed until thick, or until the eggs have doubled or even tripled in volume, about 3 minutes. With the mixer still on medium-high speed, add the granulated sugar in a slow, steady stream and continue whisking until the mixture thickens, about 2 minutes more. Using a spatula, fold in the lemon zest and vanilla until just mixed.

Sprinkle the ¾ cup/90 g flour over the egg mixture and gently fold it in. Add the melted butter and fold it in until just combined. Do not overmix.

cont'd

Spoon or pipe the batter into the prepared pans, filling each mold three-quarters full. (I use a small cup filled with batter to keep things clean and manageable; it is easier than using a spoon.) Bake, staggering the pans so that the top pan is not directly over the lower one and rotating the pans from front to back and upper to lower halfway through baking, until the edges start to turn golden brown, 12 to 14 minutes.

When the madeleines come out of the oven, turn them out onto wire racks. Dust with powdered sugar and serve immediately.

the gluten-free
basic madeleine

1¼ CUPS/200 G RICE FLOUR, PLUS MORE FOR DUSTING THE PANS

¼ CUP/35 G EXTRA-FINE CORNMEAL

1 TSP BAKING POWDER

½ TSP SALT

3 EGGS, AT ROOM TEMPERATURE

⅔ CUP/130 G SUGAR

1 TBSP HONEY

½ CUP/115 G UNSALTED BUTTER, MELTED AND COOLED TO ROOM TEMPERATURE, PLUS MORE FOR GREASING THE PANS

1 VANILLA BEAN, SPLIT LENGTHWISE AND SEEDS SCRAPED FROM THE POD (RESERVE THE POD FOR ANOTHER USE; SEE NOTE, PAGE 19)

MAKES **48** MADELEINES

NAME: *Serena Giacometti*
LOCATION: *Santa Maria di Sala, Venice, Italy*
MAD MORSEL: *This is a variation of Serena's The Basic with Vanilla Bean (page 18) that allows gluten-sensitive folks to enjoy these tasty baked treats, too. The cornmeal gives these madeleines a nice texture.*

Into a medium bowl, sift together the rice flour, cornmeal, baking powder, and salt and set aside.

In the bowl of a stand mixer fitted with the paddle attachment, beat the eggs, sugar, and honey on medium-high speed until light and fluffy and doubled in volume, about 5 minutes. Using a rubber spatula, fold the flour mixture into the egg mixture until just combined. Add the melted butter and vanilla seeds and mix until combined. Refrigerate the batter for at least 2 hours or up to 24 hours.

Position one rack in the upper quarter of the oven and another in the center and preheat to 450°F/230°C/gas 8. Generously grease two madeleine pans with butter and dust them with flour, tapping out any excess.

Spoon or pipe the batter into the prepared pans, filling each mold no more than three-quarters full. Reduce the temperature to 400°F/200°C/gas 6 and bake, staggering the pans so that the top pan is not directly over the lower one and rotating the pans from front to back and upper to lower, until the center of the

cont'd

madeleines starts to form a depression, 3 to 5 minutes. Reduce the oven temperature again, this time to 350°F/180°C/gas 4, and continue baking until the depression becomes a little hump (characteristic of all good madeleines) and the edges just start to color, about 4 minutes more.

Immediately turn out the madeleines onto a wire rack and let cool. Wipe out the pans and let cool. Re-grease and re-flour the pans, re-fill with batter, and continue baking until all the batter has been used. Serve warm or at room temperature.

CHOCOLATE MADELEINES

chocolate-
olive oil

⅓ CUP/75 ML EXTRA-VIRGIN OLIVE OIL, PLUS MORE FOR GREASING THE PANS

½ CUP/60 G ALL-PURPOSE FLOUR, PLUS MORE FOR DUSTING THE PANS

¼ CUP/20 G COCOA POWDER

½ TSP BAKING POWDER

PINCH OF SALT

2 EGGS, AT ROOM TEMPERATURE

½ CUP/100 G SUGAR

½ TSP VANILLA EXTRACT

COARSE SEA SALT FOR SPRINKLING (OPTIONAL)

MAKES 24 MADELEINES

NAME: *Gayle Gonzales*

LOCATION: *San Francisco*

MAD MORSEL: *Gayle describes the marriage of chocolate and olive oil as "a thing of unique beauty" and loves the way a generous pinch of sea salt brings out both the earthy richness of cocoa and the savory lusciousness of extra-virgin olive oil. Make sure you take care in choosing your olive oil—you want a flavor that's strong enough to stand up to the cocoa.*

Position one rack in the upper quarter of the oven and another in the center and preheat to 375°F/190°C/gas 5. Generously grease two madeleine pans with olive oil and dust with flour, tapping out any excess. Set aside.

Into a medium bowl, sift together the flour, cocoa powder, baking powder, and salt and set aside.

In a large mixing bowl, with a handheld mixer, beat the eggs on medium speed until thoroughly blended, about 1 minute. Increase the speed to medium-high, add the sugar, and beat until the mixture is thick and pale, about 3 minutes more. Add the vanilla and beat until combined. Using a rubber spatula, gently fold in the flour mixture until just combined. Fold in the olive oil.

Spoon or pipe the batter into the prepared pans, filling the molds no more than three-quarters full. Bake, staggering the pans so that the top pan is not directly over the lower one and rotating the pans from front to back and upper to lower halfway through baking, until the edges just start to color, 10 to 12 minutes.

Immediately turn out the madeleines onto a wire rack and let cool. Sprinkle with coarse sea salt (if using) while warm. Serve warm or at room temperature.

chocolate-
hazelnut

3 EGGS, AT ROOM
TEMPERATURE

½ CUP/100 G SUGAR

¾ CUP/90 G ALL-PURPOSE
FLOUR, PLUS MORE FOR
DUSTING THE PANS

3 TBSP COCOA POWDER

½ TSP BAKING POWDER

¼ TSP SALT

⅓ CUP/80 G NUTELLA
(OR OTHER CHOCOLATE-
HAZELNUT SPREAD)

1 TBSP FRANGELICO LIQUEUR
(OR OTHER HAZELNUT-
FLAVORED LIQUEUR)

MAKES
24
MADELEINES

NAME: *Mary Jaracz*
LOCATION: *Pendleton, IN*
MAD MORSEL: *Mary and her husband love Nutella so much that she often updates dessert recipes to include it as an ingredient. The hazelnut liqueur here is potent enough to prevent the Nutella from being overpowered by the chocolate.*

In a medium bowl, with a handheld mixer, beat the eggs and the sugar on medium-high speed until slightly frothy. Add the flour, 1 tbsp of the cocoa powder, the baking powder, and salt and beat on low speed until blended. Add the Nutella, Frangelico, and melted butter and beat until all the ingredients are well incorporated. Stir in the mini chocolate chips (if using).

Place a 1-gl/3.8-L plastic zip-top bag inside a large bowl. (The bowl will help hold the bag open and in place.) Pour the batter into the bag. Press out any extra air, seal the bag, and refrigerate for at least 3 hours or up to 24 hours.

Position one rack in the upper quarter of the oven and another in the center and preheat to 325°F/165°C/gas 3. Grease two madeleine pans with melted butter and dust with flour, tapping out any excess.

Cut about ½ in/12 mm off one of the bottom corners of the zip-top bag. Pipe the batter into the prepared pans, filling each mold about two-thirds full. Bake, staggering the pans so that the top pan is not directly over the lower one and rotating the pans from front to back and upper to lower halfway through baking, 16 to 20 minutes, or until the edges start turning brown.

½ CUP/115 G UNSALTED
BUTTER, MELTED AND
COOLED, PLUS MORE FOR
GREASING THE PANS

¼ CUP/45 G MINI
SEMISWEET CHOCOLATE
CHIPS (OPTIONAL)

2 TBSP POWDERED SUGAR

MELTED CHOCOLATE (SEE
PAGE 107, OPTIONAL)

CRUSHED HAZELNUTS
(OPTIONAL)

Let cool in the pans on a wire rack for 5 minutes, then turn the madeleines out onto the rack.

Meanwhile, in a small bowl, whisk together the remaining 2 tbsp cocoa powder and the powdered sugar until blended. Dust the madeleines generously with the mixture and, if desired, dip in melted chocolate and sprinkle with crushed hazelnuts. Serve immediately.

chocolate
and ginger

3/4 CUP/170 G UNSALTED BUTTER, CUT INTO SMALL PIECES, PLUS MORE, MELTED, FOR GREASING THE PAN

4 OZ/115 G DARK CHOCOLATE (70% CACAO), COARSELY CHOPPED

1 TSP INSTANT ESPRESSO POWDER

1/2 CUP/60 G ALL-PURPOSE FLOUR, PLUS MORE FOR DUSTING THE PAN

3/4 TSP BAKING SODA

2 PINCHES OF SALT

MAKES 12 MADELEINES

NAME: *Michelle Cheng*

LOCATION: *Brooklyn*

MAD MORSEL: *The unique chocolate combinations Michelle encountered on a trip to Barcelona inspired these zingy little cakes. She found the perfect balance between these two powerhouse flavors, resulting in a taste that's fresh and dark as well as tangy and nutty. If you like your madeleines with an extra kick, be sure to add the optional cayenne pepper.*

In a heat-proof bowl set over a pot of simmering water, gently melt the butter and chocolate, stirring occasionally. Stir in the espresso. When the mixture appears smooth and glossy, remove the bowl from the heat and set aside to cool.

Into a small bowl, sift together the flour, baking soda, and salt and set aside.

In a large bowl, whisk together the eggs until just broken up, about 30 seconds. Whisking vigorously, add the sugar in a slow, steady stream and continue whisking until it is completely incorporated and the mixture is about double in volume, thick, and a bit frothy, 4 to 5 minutes. (Feel free to use a stand mixer fitted with the whisk attachment or a handheld electric mixer.) Add the flour mixture in two additions, mixing just until incorporated. Fold in the melted and cooled chocolate-butter mixture, the ginger, lemon zest, and cayenne pepper (if using). Let rest for about 15 minutes.

2 EGGS, AT ROOM
TEMPERATURE

1/3 CUP/65 G SUGAR

2 TBSP PEELED AND
COARSELY GRATED FRESH
GINGER

1 TSP LEMON ZEST

1/2 TSP CAYENNE PEPPER
(OPTIONAL)

Position a rack in the center of the oven and preheat to 400°F/200°C/gas 6. Grease a madeleine pan with melted butter and dust with flour, tapping out any excess. Put the pan on a large baking sheet for easier handling.

Spoon or pipe the batter into the prepared pan, filling each mold about three-quarters full. There is no need to spread out the batter. Bake until the tops spring back when touched lightly, 12 to 15 minutes.

Immediately turn out the madeleines onto a wire rack and let cool. Serve warm or at room temperature.

spicy
chocolate

⅓ CUP/40 G ALL-PURPOSE FLOUR, PLUS MORE FOR DUSTING THE PAN

1 TSP BAKING POWDER

2 TBSP COCOA POWDER (USE YOUR FAVORITE BRAND)

¼ TSP GROUND CINNAMON

¼ TSP CHIPOTLE SEASONING

½ TSP ANCHO CHILE POWDER

2 EGGS, AT ROOM TEMPERATURE

⅓ CUP/65 G GRANULATED SUGAR

6 TBSP/85 G UNSALTED BUTTER, MELTED AND COOLED, PLUS MORE FOR GREASING THE PAN

POWDERED SUGAR (OPTIONAL)

MAKES 12 MADELEINES

NAME: *Robyn Goodwin*

LOCATION: *Northern Arizona*

MAD MORSEL: *After her two sons-in-law spent time in Mexico and developed a hankering for all things spicy, Robyn came up with these lively little treats. A hands-down favorite on her farm in Arizona, it's the perfect fix for a chocoholic in a hot climate—no melted-chocolate mess here!*

Into a small bowl, sift together the flour, baking powder, cocoa powder, and spices and set aside.

In the bowl of a stand mixer fitted with the whisk attachment, whisk together the eggs and granulated sugar until thick and pale, 2 to 4 minutes. Using a silicone spatula, gently fold in the flour mixture, followed by the melted butter, and mix until just combined. Cover with plastic wrap, pressing the wrap directly against the surface to prevent the batter from drying out, and refrigerate for at least 3 hours or up to 3 days. (This helps develop the characteristic "crown," known as the hump or the bump.)

Position a rack in the center of the oven and preheat to 400°F/200°C/gas 6. Generously grease a madeleine pan with melted butter and dust with flour, tapping out any excess.

Spoon or pipe the batter into the prepared pan, filling each mold about three-quarters full. Tap the pan lightly on the counter to remove air bubbles. Bake until the madeleines lighten and spring back when touched, 11 to 13 minutes.

Immediately turn out the madeleines onto a wire rack and let cool. Sprinkle with powdered sugar (if using). Serve warm or at room temperature.

bacon and
chocolate

¾ CUP/90 G ALL-PURPOSE FLOUR, PLUS MORE FOR DUSTING THE PANS

1 TSP BAKING POWDER

PINCH OF SALT

2 LARGE EGGS, AT ROOM TEMPERATURE

¼ CUP/50 G GRANULATED SUGAR

1 TBSP MAPLE SYRUP

2 TBSP PACKED DARK BROWN SUGAR

ZEST OF 1 ORANGE

6 TBSP/85 G UNSALTED BUTTER, MELTED AND KEPT WARM, PLUS MORE FOR GREASING THE PANS

NAME: *Sean Magrann-Wells*
LOCATION: *New York, NY*
MAD MORSEL: *Years ago, when a friend handed Sean a chocolate bar with a strip of bacon, he thought his friend was playing a prank on him. Never one to refuse a new taste, he indulged, and discovered one of his favorite flavor combinations of all time, captured here in the classic French confection.*

Into a small bowl, sift together the flour, baking powder, and salt and set aside.

In a large bowl, whisk together the eggs, granulated sugar, maple syrup, brown sugar, and orange zest until thoroughly blended. Add the flour mixture and whisk until just combined. Add the melted butter and mix until just incorporated. Cover the bowl with plastic wrap and let rest in the refrigerator for at least 1 hour or up to 24 hours.

Position one rack in the upper quarter of the oven and another in the center and preheat to 400°F/200°C/gas 6. Generously grease two madeleine pans with melted butter and dust with flour, tapping out any excess.

Spoon or pipe the batter into the prepared pans, filling each mold about two-thirds full, and bake, staggering the pans so that the top pan is not directly over the lower one, for 4 minutes. Then rotate the pans from front to back and upper to lower, reduce the heat to 350°F/180°C/gas 4, and bake until the edges are golden brown, about 5 minutes more.

cont'd

8 OZ/225 G DARK CHOCOLATE, SUCH AS GODIVA

3 STRIPS OF BACON, COOKED UNTIL CRISP AND CRUMBLED INTO SMALL PIECES

CAYENNE PEPPER (OPTIONAL)

Let the madeleines rest in the pans on a wire rack for 5 minutes, then turn them out onto the rack and let cool.

Meanwhile, in a double boiler over simmering water, melt the chocolate, stirring occasionally, until the chocolate is completely melted and smooth. Remove from the heat. Dip each madeleine into the chocolate, sprinkle with the crumbled bacon, and dust lightly with the cayenne (if using). Return to the wire rack and let set. Serve warm or at room temperature.

gluten-free
chocolate

VEGETABLE OIL FOR
GREASING THE PANS

1/3 CUP/50 G BROWN RICE
FLOUR, PLUS MORE FOR
DUSTING THE PANS

1 1/2 TBSP POTATO STARCH

2 1/2 TSP TAPIOCA FLOUR

2 TBSP COCOA POWDER

1/2 CUP/60 G GROUND
ALMONDS

1/4 TSP XANTHAN GUM

PINCH OF SALT

MAKES ABOUT
24
MADELEINES

NAME: *Luane Kohnke*
LOCATION: *New York, NY*
MAD MORSEL: *Growing up on her family's farm in Wisconsin, Luane started baking cookies when she was nine. Later on, when a friend's son was diagnosed with celiac disease, she turned her attention to gluten-free baking, and this is one of the delicious results.*

Position one rack in the upper quarter of the oven and another in the center and preheat to 325°F/165°C/gas 3. Grease two madeleine pans lightly with vegetable oil and dust with brown rice flour, tapping out any excess. Set aside.

Into a medium bowl, sift together the brown rice flour, potato starch, tapioca flour, cocoa powder, ground almonds, xanthan gum, and salt and set aside.

In the bowl of a stand mixer fitted with the paddle attachment, beat the eggs, superfine sugar, vanilla, and yogurt on medium-high speed until thick and pale, about 5 minutes. Reduce the speed to low. Add the flour mixture and beat until combined. Add the melted butter and mix until incorporated.

Spoon or pipe the batter into the prepared pans, filling each mold until halfway full. Bake, staggering the pans so that the top pan is not directly over the lower one and rotating the pans from front to back and upper to lower halfway through baking, until the madeleines spring back when lightly touched, 8 to 10 minutes.

CHOCOLATE MADELEINES
37

cont'd

3 EGGS, AT ROOM
TEMPERATURE

⅓ CUP/65 G SUPERFINE
SUGAR

½ TSP VANILLA EXTRACT

1 TSP PLAIN YOGURT

½ CUP/115 G UNSALTED
BUTTER, MELTED AND
COOLED

POWDERED SUGAR
(OPTIONAL)

Let the madeleines rest in the pans on a wire rack for a few minutes, then turn them out, shell-side up, onto the rack and let cool. Dust with powdered sugar (if using) and serve warm or at room temperature.

SPICY/NUTTY MADELEINES

honey
almond

³/₄ CUP/90 G CAKE FLOUR, PLUS MORE FOR DUSTING THE PAN

1 TSP BAKING POWDER

¹/₂ TSP SALT

4 EGGS, AT ROOM TEMPERATURE

¹/₂ CUP/100 G SUGAR

¹/₄ CUP/75 G ALMOND PASTE

2 TBSP HONEY

6 TBSP/85 G UNSALTED BUTTER, MELTED AND COOLED, PLUS MORE FOR GREASING THE PAN

¹/₂ TSP VANILLA EXTRACT

NAME: *Amy Treadwell*
LOCATION: *San Francisco*
MAD MORSEL: *These madeleines owe their light, nutty flavor and moist crumb to almond paste. They pair especially well with hot tea.*

Into a small bowl, sift together the cake flour, baking powder, and salt and set aside.

In the bowl of a stand mixer fitted with the paddle attachment, beat the eggs, sugar, and almond paste on low speed until just combined. Increase the speed to medium and beat until the mixture is light and airy and has increased in volume, 5 to 6 minutes. Reduce the speed to low, add the flour mixture, and beat until just combined. Using a rubber spatula, fold in the honey, melted butter, and vanilla until well blended. Cover the bowl with plastic wrap and refrigerate for at least 1 hour or up to 24 hours.

Position a rack in the center of the oven and preheat to 375°F/190°C/gas 5. Grease a madeleine pan with melted butter and dust with flour, tapping out any excess.

Spoon or pipe the batter into the prepared pan, filling each mold about three-quarters full. Do not smooth out the batter. Bake until the madeleines are puffed up and the edges are just starting to turn brown, 7 to 9 minutes.

Immediately turn out the madeleines onto a wire rack and let cool. Wipe out the pan and let cool. Continue preparing, filling, and baking the pan until all the batter has been used. Serve warm or at room temperature the same day they are made, but if you need to store them, stack in a wide, shallow airtight container, separating the layers with waxed paper.

vanilla
walnut

¾ CUP/90 G ALL-PURPOSE FLOUR, PLUS MORE FOR DUSTING THE PANS

½ TSP BAKING POWDER

¼ CUP/30 G FINELY CHOPPED TOASTED WALNUTS

2 LARGE EGGS, AT ROOM TEMPERATURE

½ CUP/100 G SUGAR

1 VANILLA BEAN, SPLIT LENGTHWISE AND SEEDS SCRAPED FROM THE POD (RESERVE THE POD FOR ANOTHER USE; SEE NOTE, PAGE 19)

1 TSP VANILLA EXTRACT

5 TBSP/70 G UNSALTED BUTTER, MELTED AND COOLED, PLUS MORE FOR GREASING THE PANS

MAPLE GLAZE (OPTIONAL, PAGE 112)

NAME: *Robyn Goodwin*
LOCATION: *Northern Arizona*
MAD MORSEL: *Robyn loves walnuts and vanilla, so this sweet version became her must-have madeleine—there's almost always a fresh or frozen batch in her home. Though you can use either raw or roasted walnuts, Robyn likes the hidden flavors that toasting brings out in the nuts.*

Into a medium bowl, sift together the flour and baking powder. Add the walnuts and toss until coated. Set aside.

In the bowl of a stand mixer fitted with the whisk attachment, whisk together the eggs and sugar on medium-high speed until thick and pale, 2 to 4 minutes. Add the seeds from the vanilla bean and the vanilla extract to the egg mixture. Using a spatula, gently fold in the flour mixture and then the melted butter. Cover the batter with plastic wrap, pressing the wrap directly against the surface to prevent it from drying out, and refrigerate for at least 3 hours or up to 3 days.

Position one rack in the upper quarter of the oven and another in the center and preheat to 400°F/200°C/gas 6. Generously grease two madeleine pans with melted butter and dust with flour, tapping out any excess.

MAKES
24
MADELEINES

Spoon or pipe the batter into the prepared pans, filling each mold about three-quarters full. Lightly tap the pan on the counter to remove any air bubbles. Bake, staggering the pans so that the top pan is not directly over the lower one and rotating the pans from front to back and upper to lower halfway through baking, until the madeleines are puffed and golden and spring back when lightly touched, 11 to 13 minutes.

Immediately turn out the madeleines onto a wire rack and let cool. Serve warm or at room temperature.

pistachio
cardamom

¾ CUP/90 G CAKE FLOUR, PLUS MORE FOR DUSTING THE PAN

1 TSP GROUND CARDAMOM

½ TSP BAKING POWDER

½ TSP SALT

3 EGGS, AT ROOM TEMPERATURE

½ CUP/100 G SUGAR

1 TSP VANILLA EXTRACT

5 TBSP/70 G UNSALTED BUTTER, MELTED AND COOLED TO ROOM TEMPERATURE, PLUS MORE FOR GREASING THE PAN

¼ CUP/30 G CHOPPED TOASTED PISTACHIOS

MAKES 24 MADELEINES

NAME: *Amy Treadwell*

LOCATION: *San Francisco*

MAD MORSEL: *Amy coauthored a book called* Whoopie Pies *with Sarah Billingsley. Sarah created a pistachio-cardamom whoopie pie that was a big hit, so it seemed like a good idea to try this excellent combo as a madeleine. We think it's a winner!*

Into a small bowl, sift together the cake flour, cardamom, baking powder, and salt and set aside.

In the bowl of a stand mixer fitted with the whisk attachment, whisk together the eggs, sugar, and vanilla on medium-high speed until very light and nearly double in volume, about 5 minutes.

Using a rubber spatula, fold the flour mixture and the melted butter into the egg mixture until just combined. Gently mix in the chopped pistachios. Cover the bowl with plastic wrap and refrigerate for at least 1 hour or up to 24 hours.

Position a rack in the center of the oven and preheat to 400°F/200°C/gas 6. Grease a madeleine pan with melted butter and dust with flour, tapping out any excess.

Spoon or pipe the batter into the prepared pan, filling each mold about three-quarters full. Do not smooth out the batter. Bake until the madeleines are puffed up and the edges have just started to brown, 8 to 10 minutes.

Immediately turn out the madeleines onto a wire rack and let cool. Wipe out the pan and let cool. Continue preparing, filling, and baking the pan until all the batter has been used. Serve warm or at room temperature the same day they are made.

hazelnut
brandy

½ CUP PLUS 1 TBSP/130 G
UNSALTED BUTTER

5 TBSP/40 G ALL-PURPOSE
FLOUR, PLUS MORE FOR
DUSTING THE PANS

½ CUP/50 G WHOLE
HAZELNUTS

1¼ CUPS/120 G POWDERED
SUGAR, PLUS MORE FOR
DUSTING

PINCH OF SALT

4 EGG WHITES, AT ROOM
TEMPERATURE

¼ TSP VANILLA EXTRACT

1 TBSP BRANDY

MAKES ABOUT 24 MADELEINES

NAME: *Kristen Hewitt*
LOCATION: *San Francisco*
MAD MORSEL: *At one of Kristen's annual ladies' lunches, she decided to bake cookies for her friends to take home as party favors, and delicate, ladylike madeleines seemed to be the perfect choice. She put her own spin on this Martha Stewart–originated recipe by adding brandy and removing the skins from the hazelnuts to create a smoother texture.*

In a small saucepan, melt the butter over medium-low heat and continue heating until it turns light amber in color, about 5 minutes. Let cool.

Position one rack in the upper quarter of the oven and another in the center and preheat to 275°F/135°C/gas 1. Grease two madeleine pans with 1 tbsp of the brown butter and dust lightly with flour, tapping out any excess. Set aside.

Arrange the hazelnuts in a single layer on a baking pan and toast them in the oven until they begin to release their aroma, about 12 minutes. Transfer the pan to a wire rack and let cool for about 5 minutes. The nuts should still be warm. Using a clean kitchen towel, remove the loose skins from the hazelnuts, a handful at a time, by rubbing them together in the towel. When the hazelnuts are completely cool, put them and 1 tbsp of the powdered sugar in the bowl of a food processor fitted with a steel blade, and process until very fine.

In a medium bowl, whisk together the hazelnut mixture, the remaining powdered sugar, the flour, and salt. Add the egg whites, vanilla, and brandy and whisk to combine. Add the remaining brown butter and whisk until just incorporated.

Increase the oven temperature to 350°F/180°C/gas 4. Spoon or pipe the batter into the prepared pans, filling each mold about three-quarters full. Bake, staggering the pans so that the top pan is not directly over the lower one and rotating the pans from front to back and upper to lower halfway through baking, until slightly golden, 25 to 30 minutes.

Let cool in the pans on a wire rack for a few minutes, then turn out the madeleines onto the rack to cool completely. Dust with powdered sugar for the final touch! Serve warm or at room temperature.

maple
pecan

3/4 CUP/90 G CAKE FLOUR, PLUS MORE FOR DUSTING THE PAN

1/2 TSP BAKING POWDER

1/2 TSP SALT

3 EGGS, AT ROOM TEMPERATURE

1/2 CUP/100 G SUGAR

1 TBSP PURE MAPLE SYRUP

1/4 TSP MAPLE EXTRACT (OPTIONAL)

5 TBSP/70 G UNSALTED BUTTER, MELTED AND COOLED, PLUS MORE FOR GREASING THE PAN

1/2 CUP/55 G TOASTED CHOPPED PECANS

NAME: *Amy Treadwell*
LOCATION: *San Francisco*
MAD MORSEL: *Amy is a native New Englander who loves maple in just about anything. After you taste these, we're betting you will, too.*

Into a medium bowl, sift together the cake flour, baking powder, and salt and set aside.

In the bowl of a stand mixer fitted with the paddle attachment, beat the eggs and sugar on medium-high speed until very light and nearly double in volume, about 5 minutes. Add the maple syrup and the maple extract (if using) and beat until combined.

Using a rubber spatula, fold the flour mixture and the melted butter into the egg mixture until just combined. Fold in the chopped pecans. Cover the bowl with plastic wrap and refrigerate for at least 1 hour or up to 24 hours.

Position a rack in the center of the oven and preheat to 400°F/200°C/gas 6. Grease a madeleine pan with melted butter and dust with flour, tapping out any excess.

Spoon or pipe the batter into the prepared pan, filling each mold about three-quarters full. Do not smooth out the batter. Bake until the madeleines are puffed up and the edges have just started to brown, 8 to 10 minutes.

Immediately turn out the madeleines onto a wire rack and let cool. Wipe out the pan and let cool. Continue preparing, filling, and baking the pan until all the batter has been used. Serve warm or at room temperature.

MAKES
24
MADELEINES

molasses
spice

¾ CUP/90 G ALL-PURPOSE FLOUR, PLUS MORE FOR DUSTING THE PANS

½ TSP BAKING POWDER

½ TSP GROUND CINNAMON

¼ TSP GROUND CLOVES

¼ TSP FRESHLY GROUND NUTMEG

¼ TSP SALT

3 LARGE EGGS, AT ROOM TEMPERATURE

½ CUP/100 G GRANULATED SUGAR

⅓ CUP/75 ML MOLASSES

½ CUP/115 G UNSALTED BUTTER, MELTED AND COOLED, PLUS MORE FOR GREASING THE PANS

POWDERED SUGAR FOR DUSTING

NAME: *Mary Jaracz*
LOCATION: *Pendleton, IN*
MAD MORSEL: *For these madeleines, Mary took inspiration from the original baking maven: Grandma. Her grandmother's molasses cookies left such a mark on her taste buds that she wanted to pay homage to them in these moist and fragrant madeleines, which pair wonderfully with black tea.*

In a small bowl, whisk together the flour, baking powder, cinnamon, cloves, nutmeg, and salt until blended. Set aside.

In a large bowl, using a handheld mixer, beat the eggs and granulated sugar on medium speed until slightly frothy with little bubbles, about 1 minute. Reduce the speed to low. Add the flour mixture and beat until blended. Add the molasses and melted butter and mix until well blended.

Place a 1-gl/3.8-L plastic zip-top bag inside a large bowl. (The bowl will help hold the bag open and in place.) Pour the batter into the bag. Press out any extra air, seal the bag, and refrigerate for at least 3 hours or up to 24 hours.

Position one rack in the upper quarter of the oven and another in the center and preheat to 325°F/165°C/gas 3. Grease two madeleine pans with melted butter and dust with flour, tapping out any excess.

MAKES 24 MADELEINES

Remove the batter from the refrigerator and cut ½ in/12 mm off one of the bottom corners of the zip-top bag. Pipe the batter into the prepared pans, filling each mold about two-thirds full. Bake, staggering the pans so that the top pan is not directly over the lower one and rotating the pans from front to back and upper to lower halfway through baking, until the edges have started to brown and the tops spring back when lightly touched, 18 to 23 minutes.

Let cool in the pans on a wire rack for 5 minutes, then turn out the madeleines onto the rack and let cool. Dust generously with powdered sugar and serve warm or at room temperature.

pumpkin
spice

2 EGGS, AT ROOM TEMPERATURE

2/3 CUP/130 G SUGAR

1 CUP/130 G CAKE FLOUR, PLUS MORE FOR DUSTING THE PAN

1/2 CUP/115 G UNSALTED BUTTER, MELTED AND COOLED, PLUS MORE FOR GREASING THE PAN

4 TBSP/60 ML PUMPKIN PUREE

1 TSP ORANGE JUICE

1/2 TSP GROUND CINNAMON

1/4 TSP FRESHLY GROUND NUTMEG

1/4 TSP GROUND CLOVES

1/4 TSP GROUND ALLSPICE

1/2 TSP SALT

NAME: *Miss Madeleine*

LOCATION: *Plymouth, MA*

MAD MORSEL: *Growing up in Paris, Miss Madeleine didn't experience the wonders of pumpkin pie until later in life, when her travels took her to the United States one November. Inspired, she came up with these festive madeleines—just the smell of them baking in the oven will get you thinking about the holidays!*

In the bowl of a stand mixer fitted with the paddle attachment, beat the eggs and sugar on low speed until just combined, then increase the speed to medium and beat until light and airy, 5 to 6 minutes. Still on low speed, add the flour and beat until just combined. Add the melted butter, pumpkin puree, orange juice, cinnamon, nutmeg, cloves, allspice, and salt and beat until well blended, about 2 minutes. Cover the bowl with plastic wrap, pressing the wrap directly against the surface to prevent drying out, and refrigerate the batter for at least 1 hour or up to 24 hours.

Position a rack in the center of the oven and preheat to 375°F/190°C/gas 5. Grease a madeleine pan with melted butter and dust with flour, tapping out any excess.

Spoon or pipe the batter into the prepared pan, filling each mold about three-quarters full. Do not smooth out the batter. Bake until the madeleines are puffed up and the edges have just started to brown, 8 to 10 minutes.

Immediately turn the madeleines out onto a wire rack and let cool. Wipe out the pan and let cool. Continue preparing, filling, and baking the pan until the all the batter has been used. Serve warm or at room temperature.

FRUITY MADELEINES

double-orange
with toasted coconut

3/4 CUP/90 G CAKE FLOUR, PLUS MORE FOR DUSTING THE PANS

1 TSP BAKING POWDER

1/2 TSP SALT

3 EGGS, AT ROOM TEMPERATURE

1/4 CUP/50 G GRANULATED SUGAR

4 TBSP/60 ML ORANGE JUICE

ZEST OF 1 ORANGE

6 TBSP/85 G UNSALTED BUTTER, MELTED AND COOLED, PLUS MORE FOR GREASING THE PANS

1 CUP/100 G POWDERED SUGAR

1/2 CUP/45 G TOASTED UNSWEETENED COCONUT (SEE PAGE 119)

NAME: *Miss Madeleine*
LOCATION: *Kudahuvadhoo, Maldives*
MAD MORSEL: *While cruising through the Indian Ocean, Miss Madeleine wanted to create a treat that paid homage to the local ingredients of her beloved Maldive Islands. This tangy, sweet treat is perfect for any time of year: Coconut and orange flavors transport you to tropical climes, while the luscious glaze and toasted coconut flakes look just like a wintry blanket of snow covered in ice crystals.*

Into a small bowl, sift together the cake flour, baking powder, and salt and set aside.

In the bowl of a stand mixer fitted with the paddle attachment, beat the eggs and granulated sugar on low speed until just combined, then increase the speed to medium and beat until light, airy, and doubled in volume, 5 to 6 minutes. Add the flour mixture and beat on low until just combined. Using a rubber spatula, fold in 2 tbsp of the orange juice, the orange zest, and melted butter until well blended. Cover the bowl with plastic wrap and refrigerate for at least 1 hour or up to 24 hours.

Position a rack in the upper quarter of the oven and another in the center and preheat to 375°F/190°C/gas 5. Grease two madeleine pans with melted butter and dust with flour, tapping out any excess.

MAKES 24 MADELEINES

cont'd

Spoon or pipe the batter into the prepared pans, filling each mold about three-quarters full. Do not smooth out the batter. Bake, staggering the pans so that the top pan is not directly above the lower one and rotating them back to front and upper to lower halfway through baking, until the madeleines are puffed up and the edges have just started to brown, 7 to 9 minutes. Immediately turn out the madeleines onto a wire rack and let cool.

Meanwhile, mix the powdered sugar and 1 tbsp of the remaining orange juice in a small, deep bowl until the mixture is smooth and pourable. If necessary, add more orange juice, ½ tsp at a time, to achieve the desired consistency.

When the madeleines have cooled, dip each one about halfway into the glaze, letting the excess drip off, then sprinkle with the toasted coconut. Return to the wire rack and let the glaze set, about 30 minutes.

Serve the same day they are made, but if you need to store them, stack in a wide, shallow airtight container, separating the layers with waxed paper.

orange-almond

3 EGGS, AT ROOM
TEMPERATURE

½ CUP/100 G SUGAR

6 TBSP/45 G ALL-PURPOSE
FLOUR, PLUS MORE FOR
DUSTING THE PANS

2 TBSP ALMOND MEAL
(OR ¼ CUP/30 G TOASTED
ALMONDS, COOLED AND
FINELY GROUND) (SEE NOTE)

½ CUP/115 G UNSALTED
BUTTER, MELTED AND
COOLED, PLUS 2 TBSP

1 TBSP ORANGE ZEST

MAKES
24
MADELEINES

NAME: *Lorena Jones*
LOCATION: *San Francisco*
MAD MORSEL: *Lorena grew up on an almond farm in the Central Valley of Northern California, where most of the world's almonds are grown and where eating almonds every day in every way is the norm. She still eats almonds all the time, and this recipe gives a nod to her adult love of Middle Eastern flavors while still servicing her childhood-born almond addiction.*

In the bowl of a stand mixer fitted with the whisk attachment, whisk the eggs on medium speed while adding the sugar in a slow, steady stream. Increase the speed to medium-high and continue whisking until the eggs triple in volume, turn a glossy pale yellow, and fall off the whisk in 1- to 4-in/2.5- to 10-cm ribbons that sit atop the mixture for a few seconds before melting in.

Position one rack in the upper quarter of the oven and another in the center and preheat to 400°F/200°C/gas 6.

Sift together the flour and the almond meal over the egg mixture, while gently folding it in with a large rubber spatula. Do not add more than 1 to 2 tbsp of the flour mixture until the previous addition has been completely incorporated or you will end up with deposits of flour encased in egg batter.

Pour the ½ cup/115 g melted butter through a strainer into a small mixing bowl. Add the orange zest to the butter and set aside.

Using a pastry brush, generously brush two madeleine pans with the remaining 2 tbsp melted butter and dust with flour, tapping out any excess.

Scoop 1 cup/240 ml of the batter into the bowl of melted butter. With a small spatula, gently fold the batter into the butter until completely combined. Gently fold the butter mixture into the remaining batter.

Spoon or pipe the batter into the prepared pans, filling each mold about three-quarters full. Bake, staggering the pans so that the top pan isn't directly above the lower one and rotating them from back to front and upper to lower halfway through baking, until the edges have browned slightly and the center of the madeleines spring back when gently pressed, 10 to 12 minutes.

Let cool in the pans on a wire rack for 3 minutes and then, using a butter knife, gently turn out the madeleines onto the rack and let cool. Serve warm or at room temperature.

NOTE:

To make almond meal, pulse ¼ cup/30 g whole toasted (unsalted) almonds in a food processor until very fine. No need to remove their skins. Do not overprocess, or you will wind up with almond butter.

elijah's
lemon-cocoa nib

3 EGGS, AT ROOM
TEMPERATURE

½ CUP/100 G SUGAR

¾ CUP/90 G ALL-PURPOSE
FLOUR

1 LEMON

½ CUP/115 G PLUS 2 TBSP
UNSALTED BUTTER, MELTED
AND COOLED

2 TBSP COCOA NIBS,
CHOPPED INTO TINY BITS

NAME: *Elijah Alperin*
LOCATION: *San Francisco*
MAD MORSEL: *Elijah likes these madeleines because they contain his favorite flavors—lemon and chocolate—and because his younger sister hates chocolate. His mom taught him how to make plain madeleines, and then he figured out how to add the lemon and cocoa nibs on his own.*

In a large bowl, beat the eggs with a handheld mixer on medium speed while slowly adding the sugar until the mixture is fluffy and shiny, about 5 minutes.

Sift ½ cup/60 g of the flour over the egg mixture and gently fold it in. Using a fine grater, zest the lemon directly into the batter and mix gently.

Position one rack in the upper quarter of the oven and another in the center and preheat to 400°F/200°C/gas 6. Brush two madeleine pans with the 2 tbsp melted butter and dust with the remaining ¼ cup/30 g flour, tapping out any excess. Set aside.

Gently fold 1 cup/240 ml of the batter into the remaining ½ cup/115 g melted butter until completely mixed, then return mixture to the remaining batter. Add the cocoa nibs and gently mix.

Spoon or pipe the batter into the prepared pans, filling each mold about three-quarters full. Bake, staggering the pans so that the top pan is not directly over the lower one and rotating the pans from front to back and upper to lower halfway through baking, until the madeleines are lightly browned and fully set in the middle, 10 to 12 minutes.

Let cool in the pans on a wire rack for 3 minutes, then gently turn out the madeleines onto the rack to cool completely. Serve warm or at room temperature.

lemon-
poppy seed

½ CUP/115 G UNSALTED BUTTER

1¼ CUPS/145 G ALL-PURPOSE FLOUR, PLUS MORE FOR DUSTING THE PANS

2 LARGE EGGS, AT ROOM TEMPERATURE

⅔ CUP/130 G SUGAR

2 TSP BAKING POWDER

¼ TSP BAKING SODA

¼ TSP SALT

½ CUP/120 ML SOUR CREAM

¼ CUP/60 ML HEAVY CREAM

1 TSP VANILLA EXTRACT

ZEST AND JUICE OF 1 MEYER LEMON

2 TBSP POPPY SEEDS

KIERA'S GLAZE (PAGE 111)

MAKES 48 MADELEINES

NAME: *Kiera Gilhooly*
LOCATION: *San Francisco*
MAD MORSEL: *Kiera, an avid baker and the brains behind SweetKiera.com, wanted a way to translate her favorite morning treat—lemon poppy muffins—into an any-time-of-day snack. The answer? These delicious madeleines, with their citrus burst of Meyer lemon and sweet lemon glaze.*

In a small saucepan, melt the butter over medium heat and continue heating until it turns golden brown and releases a nutty aroma, about 10 minutes. Set aside to cool.

Generously grease two madeleine pans with some of the browned butter and dust with flour, tapping out any excess. Chill the pans in the freezer for at least 1 hour or up to 3 hours. (This will help create a light, crispy outer shell that will prevent the delicate madeleines from sticking to the pan.)

In the bowl of a stand mixer fitted with the whisk attachment, beat the eggs and sugar until light, fluffy, and almost doubled in volume, about 10 minutes.

Meanwhile, in a small bowl, whisk together the flour, baking powder, baking soda, and salt. Set aside.

In a separate bowl, whisk together the sour cream, heavy cream, vanilla, and lemon zest and juice.

Sprinkle the flour mixture over the egg mixture. Using a rubber spatula, gently fold in the flour mixture until incorporated. Add the sour cream mixture and gently fold it in. Then fold in the cooled brown butter until well blended. Carefully fold in the poppy seeds until just combined. Cover the bowl with plastic wrap and refrigerate for at least 1 hour or up to 24 hours.

cont'd

Position one rack in the upper quarter of the oven and another in the center and preheat to 400°F/200°C/gas 6.

Spoon the batter into a pastry bag fitted with a large round tip or a plastic zip-top bag with ½ in/12 mm of a bottom corner cut off. Pipe the batter into the prepared pans, filling each mold about three-quarters full. Bake, staggering the pans so that the top pan is not directly over the lower one and rotating the pans from front to back and upper to lower halfway through baking, until the edges are lightly golden and a slight hump has formed in the center, 10 to 12 minutes.

Let cool in the pans on a wire rack for 5 minutes and then, using a paring knife, gently turn out the madeleines onto the rack and let cool completely. Wipe out the pans and let cool. Continue preparing, filling, and baking the pans until all the batter has been used.

When the madeleines have cooled, gently dip each one into the glaze, letting the excess drip off into the bowl. Place on parchment paper, shell-side up, and let rest until the glaze has set, about 30 minutes. These are best served the same day, but they can be stored in an airtight container at room temperature for up to 3 days.

key lime

3/4 CUP/90 G ALL-PURPOSE FLOUR, PLUS MORE FOR DUSTING THE PANS

1/2 TSP BAKING POWDER

2 LARGE EGGS, AT ROOM TEMPERATURE

1/2 CUP/100 G SUGAR

ZEST AND JUICE FROM 3 KEY LIMES OR REGULAR LIMES IF KEY LIMES ARE NOT AVAILABLE, PLUS MORE ZEST FOR GARNISH (OPTIONAL)

5 TBSP/70 G UNSALTED BUTTER, MELTED AND COOLED, PLUS MORE FOR GREASING THE PANS

MELTED CHOCOLATE (OPTIONAL, SEE PAGE 107)

MAKES 24 MADELEINES

NAME: *Robyn Goodwin*

LOCATION: *Northern Arizona*

MAD MORSEL: *Summer is the perfect time for these Key lime madeleines. They're just the right thing to bring to a picnic, barbecue, or any summer fiesta. The sweet chocolate softens the tart Key lime flavor, but for festive occasions, Robyn gives the madeleines an extra kick with a tequila-based glaze. Olé!*

Into a small bowl, sift together the flour and baking powder and set aside.

In a large bowl, using a handheld mixer, beat together the eggs and sugar on medium speed until thick and pale, 2 to 4 minutes. Whisk in the lime zest and juice.

Using a silicone spatula, gently fold the flour mixture into the egg mixture, followed by the melted butter. Cover the bowl with plastic wrap, pressing the wrap directly against the surface to prevent drying out, and refrigerate for at least 3 hours or up to 3 days.

Position one rack in the upper quarter of the oven and another in the center and preheat to 400°F/200°C/gas 6. Generously grease two madeleine pans with melted butter and dust with flour, tapping out any excess.

cont'd

Spoon or pipe the batter into the prepared pans, filling each mold about three-quarters full. Lightly tap the pans on the counter to remove any air bubbles. Bake, staggering the pans so that the top pan is not directly over the lower one and rotating the pans from front to back and upper to lower halfway through baking, until the madeleines are puffed and golden and spring back when lightly touched, 11 to 13 minutes. Immediately turn out the madeleines onto a wire rack and let cool completely.

If desired, when the madeleines have cooled, dip each one halfway into the melted chocolate, sprinkle with lime zest, and return to the rack until the glaze has set, about 30 minutes. Serve warm or at room temperature.

glazed
mango lassi

1¼ CUPS/170 G CAKE
FLOUR, PLUS MORE FOR
DUSTING THE PAN

1 TSP BAKING POWDER

½ TSP SALT

3 EGGS, AT ROOM
TEMPERATURE

¼ CUP/50 G GRANULATED
SUGAR

¼ CUP/60 ML PLUS 2 TBSP
MANGO NECTAR

¼ CUP/60 ML PLAIN GREEK-
STYLE YOGURT

6 TBSP/85 G UNSALTED
BUTTER, MELTED AND
COOLED, PLUS MORE FOR
GREASING THE PAN

½ TSP VANILLA EXTRACT

½ CUP/85 G CHOPPED
DRIED MANGO

1 CUP/100 G POWDERED
SUGAR

NAME: *Miss Madeleine*
LOCATION: *Mumbai, India*
MAD MORSEL: *During Miss Madeleine's summer in India, mango lassis served as Miss Madeleine's savior from the sweltering heat. Once the weather cooled down, she wanted a way to transform the refreshing drink into a baked treat, and this madeleine was the sweetly fragrant result.*

Into a small bowl, sift together the cake flour, baking powder, and salt and set aside.

In the bowl of a stand mixer fitted with the paddle attachment, beat the eggs and granulated sugar on low speed until just combined, then increase the speed to medium and beat until the mixture is light and airy and has doubled in volume, 5 to 6 minutes. Reduce the speed to low, add the flour mixture, and beat until just combined. Using a rubber spatula, fold in the ¼ cup/60 ml mango nectar, the yogurt, melted butter, and vanilla until well blended. Add the dried mango and stir until just combined. Cover the bowl with plastic wrap and refrigerate for at least 1 hour or up to 24 hours.

Position a rack in the center of the oven and preheat to 375°F/190°C/gas 5. Grease a madeleine pan with melted butter and dust with flour, tapping out any excess.

MAKES ABOUT
24
MADELEINES

Spoon or pipe the batter into the prepared pan, filling each mold about three-quarters full. Do not smooth out the batter. Bake until the madeleines are puffed up and the edges have just started to brown, 7 to 9 minutes.

Immediately turn out the madeleines onto a wire rack to cool. Wipe out the pan and let cool. Continue preparing, filling, and baking the pan until all the batter has been used.

Meanwhile, mix the powdered sugar and 1 tbsp of the remaining mango nectar in a small, deep bowl until the mixture is smooth and pourable. If necessary, add more mango nectar, ½ tsp at a time, to achieve the desired consistency.

When the madeleines have cooled, dip each one about halfway into the glaze, letting the excess drip off. Return to the wire rack and let the glaze set, about 30 minutes.

Serve the same day, but if you need to store them, stack in a wide, shallow airtight container, separating the layers with waxed paper.

banana bread

2 EGGS, AT ROOM
TEMPERATURE

2/3 CUP/130 G PACKED
LIGHT BROWN SUGAR

1 CUP/115 G ALL-PURPOSE
FLOUR, PLUS MORE FOR
DUSTING THE PANS

1 TSP GROUND CINNAMON

1/2 TSP SALT

1/2 CUP/115 G BUTTER,
MELTED AND COOLED,
PLUS MORE FOR GREASING
THE PANS

1/4 CUP/60 G MASHED,
RIPE BANANA

NAME: *Lara Starr*

LOCATION: *San Francisco*

MAD MORSEL: *These little cakes are a tribute to "Mimi," Lara's great-grandmother. Lara spent her childhood Sundays playing cards at Mimi's house, while Mimi served up her moist, dense banana bread. "I've never been able to get my banana bread quite as banana-y as hers," Lara says, but Mimi would probably approve of this fresh take on a classic treat.*

In a stand mixer fitted with the whisk attachment, whisk together the eggs and brown sugar on medium-high speed until the mixture has thickened and the sugar has dissolved, about 5 minutes. When the whisk is lifted, the mixture should ribbon into the bowl. Reduce the speed to low. Add the flour, cinnamon, and salt and mix just until combined. With the mixer on medium speed, add the melted butter and banana and mix until blended, 2 to 3 minutes. Cover the bowl with plastic wrap, pressing the wrap directly onto the surface of the batter, and refrigerate for at least 1 hour or overnight.

Position one rack in the upper quarter of the oven and another in the center and preheat to 375°F/190°C/gas 5. Grease two madeleine pans with melted butter and dust with flour, tapping out any excess.

Spoon the batter into the prepared pans, filling each mold about three-quarters full. Bake, staggering the pans so that the top pan is not directly above the lower one and rotating them back to front and upper to lower halfway through baking, until the edges are brown and a toothpick stuck into the highest part of the "bump" comes out clean, 10 to 12 minutes.

Immediately turn out the madeleines onto a wire rack to cool. Serve warm or at room temperature.

peanut butter
and banana

½ CUP/115 G BUTTER, MELTED AND COOLED, PLUS MORE FOR GREASING THE PANS

¼ CUP/70 G PEANUT BUTTER

¼ CUP/60 G MASHED, RIPE BANANA

2 EGGS, AT ROOM TEMPERATURE

⅔ CUP/130 G SUGAR

1 CUP/115 G ALL-PURPOSE FLOUR, PLUS MORE FOR DUSTING THE PANS

½ TSP SALT

MAKES ABOUT **24** MADELEINES

NAME: *Lara Starr*
LOCATION: *San Francisco*
MAD MORSEL: *It's become a bit of a cliché to make fun of Elvis for his peanut butter and banana sandwiches, but the King was definitely on to something.*

In a small bowl, combine the melted butter, peanut butter, and banana and stir until smooth. Set aside.

In the bowl of a stand mixer fitted with the whisk attachment, whisk together the eggs and sugar on high speed until the mixture has thickened and the sugar has dissolved, about 5 minutes. Reduce the speed to low. Add the flour and the salt and mix just until combined. With the mixer on medium speed, add the peanut butter mixture and mix until just combined, 2 to 3 minutes. Cover the bowl with plastic wrap, pressing the wrap directly onto the surface of the batter, and refrigerate for at least 1 hour or overnight.

Position a rack in the center of the oven and preheat to 375°F/190°C/gas 5. Grease two madeleine pans with melted butter and gently dust with flour, tapping out any excess.

Spoon the batter into the pans, filling each mold about three-quarters full. Bake, staggering the pans so that the top pan is not directly above the lower one and rotating them back to front and upper to lower halfway through baking, until the edges are brown and a toothpick stuck into the highest part of the "bump" comes out clean, 10 to 12 minutes.

Immediately turn the madeleines out onto a wire rack and let cool. Serve warm or at room temperature.

apple-buckwheat
with sea-salt caramel

2/3 CUP/80 G ALL-PURPOSE FLOUR, PLUS MORE FOR DUSTING THE PAN

1/4 CUP/30 G BUCKWHEAT FLOUR

1/2 TSP BAKING POWDER

1/2 TSP GROUND CINNAMON

PINCH OF SEA SALT

1/4 CUP/55 G FINELY SHREDDED APPLE OR APPLESAUCE

2 LARGE EGGS, AT ROOM TEMPERATURE

1/3 CUP/65 G SUGAR

6 TBSP/85 G UNSALTED BUTTER, MELTED AND COOLED, PLUS MORE FOR GREASING THE PAN

1/4 CUP/60 ML SEA-SALT CARAMEL (PAGE 115)

MAKES ABOUT 12 MADELEINES

NAME: *Sarah Billingsley*

LOCATION: *San Francisco*

MAD MORSEL: *This madeleine is inspired by the buckwheat crêpes, apple desserts, and sea salts typical of northern coastal France. And filling a madeleine may be unorthodox, but all Sarah can say is: If Dorie Greenspan can do it, it's legit. (You won't regret Googling her marshmallow-filled chocolate madeleine recipe.) Salted caramel pushes this delicate cake into a realm of delicious that will haunt your dreams, but if you decide not to mess with boiling sugar, remember to add a pinch of salt to your batter.*

Into a medium bowl, sift together the all-purpose flour, buckwheat flour, baking powder, cinnamon, and sea salt. If using shredded apple, add now and toss gently to combine. Set aside.

In the bowl of a stand mixer fitted with the whisk attachment, whisk together the eggs and sugar on high speed until the mixture has thickened and the sugar has dissolved, about 5 minutes. Using a rubber spatula or wooden spoon, gently fold in the flour mixture until just combined, then add the melted butter. If using applesauce, add now and fold again. Let the batter rest, covered with plastic wrap, for at least 3 hours or up to 2 days (refrigerate if resting beyond 3 hours).

Position a rack in the center of the oven and preheat to 400°F/200°C/gas 6. Generously grease the madeleine pan with melted butter and dust lightly with flour, tapping out any excess.

Spoon or pipe the batter into the prepared pan, filling each mold three-quarters full. Bake until the madeleines spring back when touched, 10 to 12 minutes.

Let cool in the pans on a wire rack for 3 minutes, and then, using a butter knife or your fingers, gently turn out the madeleines onto the rack and let cool to just-warm or room temperature before filling.

To fill the madeleines, fit a small pastry bag with a small, plain tip and spoon the caramel into the bag. Insert the pointed end of the tip into the large (unscalloped) end of the madeleine and squeeze the bag gently. The caramel will ooze from the bag into the pores of the cake; stop before the caramel begins to ooze out, or you'll end up with a sticky sugar bomb. If this is too labor intensive, turn your cakes scalloped-side up and generously drizzle them with the caramel. Enjoy these cakes the same day they are made.

cherry-cornmeal

3/4 CUP/90 G CAKE FLOUR, PLUS MORE FOR DUSTING THE PAN

1/2 CUP/70 G CORNMEAL

1/2 TSP SALT

4 EGGS, AT ROOM TEMPERATURE

1 CUP/200 G SUGAR

1 TSP ORANGE JUICE

1/2 TSP ORANGE ZEST

3/4 CUP/170 G UNSALTED BUTTER, MELTED AND COOLED, PLUS MORE FOR GREASING THE PAN

1/2 CUP/85 G CHOPPED DRIED CHERRIES

CITRUS SYRUP (PAGE 113)

NAME: *Amy Treadwell*
LOCATION: *San Francisco*
MAD MORSEL: *Of all the great bakeries in San Francisco, Arizmendi tops Amy's list—especially for its irresistible cherry cornmeal scones. The sweet fruit and crunchy cornmeal texture struck her as ideal elements for a madeleine. After some experimentation she came up with this recipe— and now, when she can't make it over to Arizmendi for a scone fix, she has a homespun variation that delivers a whole new kind of delicious.*

Into a small bowl, sift together the cake flour, cornmeal, and salt and set aside.

In the bowl of a stand mixer fitted with the whisk attachment, whisk together the eggs and sugar on medium-high speed until very light and nearly double in volume, about 5 minutes. Using a rubber spatula, fold the flour mixture, orange juice, and orange zest into the egg mixture until just combined. Stir in the butter gently. Fold in the dried cherries. Cover the bowl with plastic wrap and refrigerate for at least 1 hour or up to 24 hours.

Position a rack in the center of the oven and preheat to 400°F/200°C/gas 6. Grease a madeleine pan with melted butter and dust with flour, tapping out any excess.

Spoon or pipe the batter into the prepared pan, filling each mold about three-quarters full. Bake until the madeleines are puffed up and the edges have just started to brown, 8 to 10 minutes.

Immediately turn out the madeleines onto a wire rack and let cool. Wipe out the pan and let cool. Continue preparing, filling, and baking the pans until all the batter has been used.

In a small saucepan, gently warm the citrus syrup over low heat. Brush the warm syrup over the scalloped side of each madeleine and let it soak in. Repeat and serve immediately.

SAVORY
MADELEINES

chorizo

¾ CUP/90 G ALL-PURPOSE FLOUR, PLUS MORE FOR DUSTING THE PAN

¾ TSP BAKING POWDER

¼ TSP *PIMENT D'ESPELETTE* OR *PIMENTÓN DE LA VERA* (*DULCE*)

⅛ TSP SEA SALT

2 LARGE EGGS, AT ROOM TEMPERATURE

⅓ CUP/65 G SUGAR

3 TBSP UNSALTED BUTTER, MELTED AND COOLED, PLUS MORE FOR GREASING THE PAN

2 TBSP EXTRA-VIRGIN OLIVE OIL

¼ CUP/30 G FINELY CHOPPED SPANISH-STYLE DRY CHORIZO (OR *SAUCISSON SEC*)

2 TBSP MINCED SCALLIONS OR CHIVES (OPTIONAL)

NAME: *Stephanie Galinson*
LOCATION: *San Francisco*
MAD MORSEL: *Stephanie scoffs at the idea that madeleines are just for Proust, tea, and quiet afternoons. She whips these up for tapas-style meals or cocktail party hors d'oeuvres, or even toasts them in the morning to make a quick and hearty breakfast! You can easily double or triple this recipe if you want to serve a crowd.* Pimentón *is Spanish smoked paprika, and this recipe calls for* dulce, *the sweet and mild variety.*

Into a small bowl, sift together the flour, baking powder, *piment d'Espelette*, and salt and set aside.

In the bowl of a stand mixer fitted with the whisk attachment, whisk together the eggs and sugar on medium-high speed until thick and pale yellow, about 4 minutes.

Switch from the whisk to the paddle attachment, add the flour mixture, and beat on low speed until just combined. With the mixer running, pour in the melted butter and olive oil and mix just until incorporated. Using a rubber spatula, gently fold in the chopped chorizo and scallions (if using). Do not overmix, or the madeleines will be tough.

Pour the batter into a bowl or pitcher and cover with plastic wrap, pressing the wrap directly onto the surface of the batter to keep out air. Refrigerate for at least 3 hours or up to 24 hours. (This rest time allows the dry ingredients to fully absorb the eggs.)

MAKES 12 MADELEINES

cont'd

Position a rack in the center of the oven and preheat to 400°F/200°C/gas 6. Grease a madeleine pan with melted butter and dust with flour, tapping out any excess. Put the pan on a baking sheet for easier handling.

Spoon or pipe the batter into the prepared pan, filling each mold about three-quarters full. Bake until the madeleines are golden brown and spring back when touched, about 12 minutes.

Immediately turn out the madeleines onto a wire rack and let cool. Serve warm or at room temperature within several hours.

moroccan

3/4 CUP/90 G ALL-PURPOSE
FLOUR, PLUS MORE FOR
DUSTING THE PAN

1 TSP BAKING POWDER

2 PINCHES OF SALT

2 LARGE EGGS, AT ROOM
TEMPERATURE

3 TBSP SUGAR

3 TBSP HONEY

ZEST OF ½ LEMON

ZEST OF ½ ORANGE

6 TBSP/85 G UNSALTED
BUTTER, MELTED AND KEPT
WARM

NONSTICK COOKING SPRAY

4 EGG WHITES, AT ROOM
TEMPERATURE

2 PRESERVED LEMONS, CUT
INTO CHUNKS

NAME: *Sean Magrann-Wells*
LOCATION: *Manhattan*
MAD MORSEL: *Sean has long loved Moroccan cuisine, but his interest was recently reignited by a new fascination with preserved lemon. Its unique one-two punch of tang and sweetness make it a challenging and fun ingredient, perfectly complemented by the sun-dried tomatoes here. (For a new twist with a similar savory effect, try substituting roasted red peppers for the sun-dried tomatoes.) You can find preserved lemons at gourmet groceries like Whole Foods.*

Into a small bowl, sift together the flour, baking powder, and 1 pinch of salt. Set aside.

In a large bowl, whisk together the eggs, 2 tbsp of the sugar, 1 tbsp of the honey, and both citrus zests. Add the flour mixture and whisk until just combined. Add the melted butter and stir until just incorporated. Cover the bowl with plastic wrap and refrigerate for 1 hour or up to 24 hours.

About 30 minutes before you are ready to bake, remove the batter from refrigerator and bring it to room temperature.

Position a rack in the center of the oven and preheat to 400°F/200°C/gas 6. Coat a madeleine pan with nonstick cooking spray and dust with flour, tapping out any excess.

In a medium bowl, whisk together the egg whites, the remaining pinch of salt, and the remaining 1 tbsp sugar until soft peaks form. In a blender or food processor, combine the preserved lemons, sun-dried tomatoes, remaining 1 tbsp honey, thyme, turmeric, and canola oil and process until a paste is formed. Fold the paste gently into the egg whites.

1/3 CUP/90 G SUN-DRIED TOMATOES

2 TBSP FRESH THYME, CHOPPED

1 TBSP TURMERIC

1 TBSP CANOLA OIL

When you are ready to bake, add the egg white mixture to the room-temperature batter and fold gently until combined. Spoon or pipe the batter into the prepared pan, filling each mold two-thirds full. Bake for 4 minutes. Rotate the pan front to back, reduce the heat to 350°F/180°C/gas 4, and bake for an additional 4 minutes, or until the edges are golden brown.

Let the madeleines cool in the pan on a wire rack for 5 minutes, or until they are cool enough to remove from the molds. Using a knife to loosen the edges, carefully turn out the madeleines onto the rack and let cool before serving.

smoked paprika
and fontina

1¼ CUPS/145 G ALL-PURPOSE FLOUR, PLUS MORE FOR DUSTING THE PAN

1½ TSP SMOKED PAPRIKA

1 TSP SALT

½ TSP BAKING POWDER

¼ TSP BAKING SODA

2 EGGS, AT ROOM TEMPERATURE

¾ CUP/180 ML BUTTERMILK

½ CUP/55 G GRATED FONTINA CHEESE

5 TBSP/70 G BUTTER, MELTED AND COOLED, PLUS MORE FOR GREASING THE PAN

SMOKED SEA SALT, FOR SPRINKLING (OPTIONAL)

NAME: *Miss Madeleine*

LOCATION: *Valais, Switzerland*

MAD MORSEL: *While at her cozy chalet in the Alps, Miss Madeleine's favorite après-ski treat was cheese fondue. Wanting to replicate those delicious dipped treats in madeleine form, she used the earthy, subtly flavored fontina and added a generous dose of smoked paprika, creating a cookie with a flavor kick that's equally delicious in the lodge or in your kitchen.*

Into a small bowl, sift together the flour, paprika, salt, baking powder, and baking soda and set aside.

In the bowl of a stand mixer fitted with the whisk attachment, whisk the eggs on medium-high speed until very light and nearly double in volume, about 5 minutes. Using a rubber spatula, fold in the flour mixture, buttermilk, and fontina until just combined. Stir in the butter gently. Cover the bowl with plastic wrap, pressing the wrap directly onto the surface of the batter to keep out air, and refrigerate for at least 1 hour or up to 24 hours.

Position a rack in the center of the oven and preheat to 375°F/190°C/gas 5. Grease a madeleine pan with melted butter and dust with flour, tapping out any excess.

Spoon or pipe the filling into the prepared pan, filling each mold about three-quarters full. Sprinkle with the smoked salt (if using). Bake until the madeleines are puffed up and the edges have just started to brown, 8 to 10 minutes.

Immediately turn out the madeleines onto a wire rack and let cool. Wipe out the pan and let cool. Continue preparing, filling, and baking the pan until all the batter has been used. Serve warm or at room temperature the same day they are made.

ricotta
with tomato jam

3 TBSP ALL-PURPOSE FLOUR, PLUS MORE FOR DUSTING THE PAN

½ TSP BAKING POWDER

2 PINCHES OF SALT

1 LARGE EGG, AT ROOM TEMPERATURE

1 TBSP PACKED LIGHT BROWN SUGAR

ZEST OF 1 LEMON

3 TBSP UNSALTED BUTTER, MELTED AND KEPT WARM, PLUS MORE FOR GREASING THE PAN

NONSTICK COOKING SPRAY

NAME: *Sean Magrann-Wells*
LOCATION: *New York, NY*
MAD MORSEL: *Thinking about a savory madeleine, Sean knew his recipe would have to involve cheese, but he wanted to make sure that the result retained the light fluffiness that is so important to madeleines. Ricotta seemed like the perfect solution, and also provided a touch of sweetness that Sean sets off with a few cranks of cracked black pepper. Serve it with Tomato Jam.*

Into a small bowl, sift together the flour, baking powder, and salt and set aside.

In a medium bowl, combine the egg, brown sugar, and lemon zest and whisk together until thoroughly combined. Add the flour mixture and whisk until just combined. Add the melted butter and whisk until just incorporated. Cover the bowl with plastic wrap and refrigerate for 1 hour or up to 24 hours.

About 30 minutes before you are ready to bake, remove the batter from the refrigerator and let it come to room temperature.

Position a rack in the center of the oven and preheat to 400°F/200°C/gas 6. Coat a madeleine pan with nonstick cooking spray and dust with flour, tapping out any excess.

cont'd

3/4 TSP CRACKED BLACK PEPPER

1/2 CUP/110 G RICOTTA CHEESE

1/2 TBSP EXTRA-VIRGIN OLIVE OIL

TOMATO JAM (PAGE 117)

Fold the pepper, ricotta, and olive oil into the batter. Spoon or pipe the batter into the prepared pan, filling each mold two-thirds full. Bake for 4 minutes. Rotate the pan from front to back, lower the temperature to 350°F/180°C/gas 4, and continue baking until the madeleines are golden brown around the edges, 4 minutes more.

Let the madeleines cool in the pan on a wire rack for 5 minutes, or until they are cool enough to remove from the molds. Wipe out the pan and let cool. Continue preparing, filling, and baking the pan until all the batter has been used. Serve warm or at room temperature with the jam.

rosemary
polenta

NAME: *Miss Madeleine*
LOCATION: *Rome, Italy*
MAD MORSEL: *A brief trip to Rome turned into a months-long sojourn when Miss Madeleine ignited a torrid, whirlwind affair with a dashing Italian diplomat. Although their love story didn't have a "happily ever after," this recipe, with flavors inspired by their many alfresco dinners, serves as a delicious celebration of their passion.*

¾ CUP/90 G ALL-PURPOSE FLOUR, PLUS MORE FOR DUSTING THE PAN

½ CUP/70 G CORNMEAL

1 TSP SALT

½ TSP BAKING POWDER

½ TSP BAKING SODA

2 EGGS, AT ROOM TEMPERATURE

¾ CUP/180 ML BUTTERMILK

¼ CUP/30 G GRATED PARMIGIANO-REGGIANO CHEESE

½ TSP FINELY CHOPPED FRESH ROSEMARY

6 TBSP/85 G BUTTER, MELTED AND COOLED, PLUS MORE FOR GREASING THE PAN

MAKES 24 MADELEINES

Into a small bowl, sift together the flour, cornmeal, salt, baking powder, and baking soda and set aside.

In the bowl of a stand mixer fitted with the whisk attachment, whisk the eggs on medium-high speed until very light and nearly double in volume, about 5 minutes. Using a rubber spatula, fold the flour mixture, buttermilk, Parmigiano-Reggiano, and rosemary into the egg mixture until just combined. Stir in the butter gently. Cover the bowl with plastic wrap and refrigerate for at least 1 hour and up to 24 hours.

Position a rack in the center of the oven and preheat to 400°F/200°C/gas 6. Grease a madeleine pan with melted butter and dust with flour, tapping out any excess.

Spoon or pipe the batter into the prepared pan, filling each mold about three-quarters full. Bake until the madeleines are puffed up and the edges have just started to brown, 8 to 10 minutes.

Immediately turn out the madeleines onto a wire rack and let cool. Wipe out the pan and let cool. Continue preparing, filling, and baking the pan until all the batter has been used. Serve warm or at room temperature the same day they are made.

SPECIALTY MADELEINES

vanilla malt

2 EGGS, AT ROOM
TEMPERATURE

2/3 CUP/130 G SUGAR

1 TSP VANILLA EXTRACT

1 CUP/115 G ALL-PURPOSE
FLOUR, PLUS MORE FOR
DUSTING THE PANS

1/4 CUP/20 G MALTED MILK
POWDER

1/2 CUP/115 G UNSALTED
BUTTER, MELTED AND
COOLED, PLUS MORE FOR
GREASING THE PANS

MAKES ABOUT
24
MADELEINES

NAME: *Lara Starr*

LOCATION: *San Francisco*

MAD MORSEL: *Forget the Blarney Stone and Guinness pints—the highlight of Lara's first trip to Ireland was a little red bag of Maltesers. "This is what American malted milk balls wish they could be," she thought on her first bite. Since then, her kitchen has never been without an industrial-size can of malted milk powder, and she incorporates that same rich, nutty flavor into her baking at every opportunity.*

In a stand mixer fitted with the whisk attachment, whisk together the eggs, sugar, and vanilla on medium-high speed until the mixture is thick and the sugar has dissolved, about 5 minutes. When the whisk is lifted, the mixture should ribbon into the bowl. Reduce the speed to low. Add the flour and malted milk powder and mix just until combined. Add the melted butter and mix on medium speed until incorporated, 2 to 3 minutes. Cover the bowl with plastic wrap, pressing it directly onto the surface of the batter, and refrigerate for at least 1 hour or overnight.

Position one rack in the upper quarter of the oven and another in the center and preheat to 375°F/190°C/gas 5. Brush two madeleine pans with melted butter and gently dust with flour, tapping out any excess.

Spoon the batter into the prepared pans, filling each mold about three-quarters full. Bake, staggering the pans so that the top pan is not directly above the lower one and rotating them back to front and upper to lower halfway through baking, until the edges are brown and a toothpick stuck into the highest part of the "bump" comes out clean, 10 to 12 minutes.

Immediately turn out the madeleines onto a wire rack and let cool. Serve warm or at room temperature.

double
espresso

1/4 CUP/30 G UNBLEACHED ALL-PURPOSE FLOUR, PLUS MORE FOR DUSTING THE PAN

1/4 CUP/30 G ALMOND MEAL (OR 1/2 CUP/60 G TOASTED ALMONDS, COOLED AND FINELY GROUND) (SEE NOTE, PAGE 59)

3/4 TSP BAKING POWDER

2 TBSP FRESHLY GROUND COFFEE BEANS (NOT INSTANT)

2 PINCHES OF SEA SALT

2 GRINDS OF BLACK PEPPER

2 LARGE EGGS, AT ROOM TEMPERATURE

1/2 CUP/100 G SUPERFINE SUGAR

1/4 CUP/55 G UNSALTED BUTTER, MELTED AND COOLED, PLUS MORE FOR GREASING THE PAN

NAME: *Peter Perez*

LOCATION: *Emeryville, CA*

MAD MORSEL: *The inspiration for Peter's blasphemously Italianized madeleines didn't come simply from their most prominent flavoring. He wanted to replicate the flavor of biscotti, which he loves to eat (almost as much as he does madeleines) while sipping a caffe Americano or a cup of coffee from a French press. Using fresh coffee beans that are ground in a burr grinder will give you the best flavor. (Peter likes to use Brazilian and Kenyan beans from his local roasters Four Barrel and Sightglass.)*

Into a small bowl, sift together the flour, almond meal, and baking powder. Add the ground coffee, sea salt, and pepper and whisk until blended.

In a medium bowl, with a handheld mixer, beat the eggs and superfine sugar on medium speed until well blended, about 8 minutes. Increase the speed to medium-high and continue beating until the mixture has doubled in volume, 4 to 5 minutes. Using a rubber spatula, gently fold in the flour mixture, in three additions until just incorporated. Add the butter and mix gently until blended.

Position a rack in the center of the oven and preheat to 375°F/190°C/gas 5. Grease a nonstick madeleine pan with melted butter and dust with flour, tapping out any excess. Set aside.

MAKES ABOUT 18 MADELEINES

Spoon or pipe the batter into the prepared pan, filling each mold three-quarters full. Make sure you don't overfill. Bake until the madeleines are puffed up and slightly browned, 10 to 12 minutes. They should bounce back slightly when gently pressed in the center.

Place a clean, smooth cotton kitchen towel on a work surface. When the madeleines are done, tap the pan gently and turn them out onto the towel. Let cool, scalloped-side up, for a few minutes. Let the pan cool and wipe clean. Continue preparing, filling, and baking the pan until all the batter has been used. Serve warm.

mama's
brown butter
and bourbon

½ CUP/115 G PLUS 2 TBSP UNSALTED BUTTER

3 EGGS, AT ROOM TEMPERATURE

½ CUP/100 G SUGAR

ALL-PURPOSE FLOUR FOR DUSTING THE PANS

GENEROUS ½ CUP/60 G CAKE FLOUR OR OTHER LOW-PROTEIN (7% TO 9%) FLOUR

GENEROUS 1 TBSP MAKER'S MARK OR YOUR FAVORITE BOURBON, PLUS MORE FOR SERVING AS AN ACCOMPANIMENT (OPTIONAL)

MAKES 24 MADELEINES

NAME: *Lorena Jones*
LOCATION: *San Francisco*
MAD MORSEL: *Lorena's three children are mad for madeleines, probably because that was their coffee shop treat every time Lorena refueled with java. Eventually, they got her into the habit of making them on Sunday afternoons. One day last fall she decided to add a shot of her favorite bourbon and turned a kids' favorite into a mother's respite.*

In a small saucepan, melt the ½ cup/115 g butter over low heat until completely melted. Increase the heat just a bit (but not to medium) and swirl the pan while the butter browns. When the butter begins to release a nutty aroma and turns a toasty brown color, remove the pan from the heat and set aside to cool.

In the bowl of a stand mixer fitted with the whisk attachment, whisk the eggs on medium speed while adding the sugar in a slow, steady stream. Increase the speed to medium-high and whisk until the mixture triples in volume, turns a glossy pale yellow, and falls off the whisk in 1- to 4-in/2.5- to 10-cm ribbons that sit atop the mixture for a few seconds before melting in.

Position one rack in the upper quarter of the oven and another in the center and preheat to 400°F/200°C/gas 6. Generously grease two madeleine pans with the remaining 2 tbsp butter and dust with all-purpose flour, tapping out any excess.

Sift the cake flour over the egg mixture while gently folding it in with a large rubber spatula. Do not add more than 1 to 2 tbsp flour until the previous addition has been completely incorporated, or you will end up with deposits of flour encased in egg batter.

Pour the brown butter through a strainer into a small mixing bowl. Stir in the bourbon. Scoop 1 cup/240 ml of the batter into the bowl of brown butter and bourbon. Using a small spatula, gently fold the batter into the butter until completely combined. Gently fold the brown butter mixture into the remaining batter.

Spoon or pipe the batter into the prepared pans, filling each mold to just below the top. Bake, staggering the pans so that the top pan isn't directly above the lower one and rotating them back to front and upper to lower halfway through baking, until the edges have browned slightly and the center of the madeleines spring back when gently pressed, 10 to 12 minutes.

Let cool in the pans on a wire rack for 3 minutes and then, using a butter knife, gently turn out the madeleines onto the rack and let cool. Serve warm and wash them down with two fingers of bourbon, if desired.

matcha

¼ CUP/55 G UNSALTED BUTTER, MELTED AND COOLED, PLUS MORE FOR GREASING THE PANS

⅔ CUP/80 G ALL-PURPOSE FLOUR, PLUS MORE FOR DUSTING THE PANS

1½ TSP MATCHA, PLUS MORE FOR GARNISHING (OPTIONAL)

2 EGGS, AT ROOM TEMPERATURE

⅓ CUP/65 G GRANULATED SUGAR

PINCH OF SALT

½ TSP VANILLA EXTRACT

ZEST OF ½ LEMON

POWDERED SUGAR (OPTIONAL)

MAKES 24 MADELEINES

NAME: *Cat Grishaver*
LOCATION: *Portland, OR*
MAD MORSEL: *The distinctive soft green shade of these madeleines satisfies Cat's artistic eye, but their pleasure isn't just aesthetic; these yummy little cakes pack a flavor punch of bright green tea, softened just enough by lemon, butter, and vanilla.*

Grease two madeleine pans with melted butter and dust with flour, tapping out any excess. Chill the pans in the freezer until ready to bake. (This helps the madeleines pop out of the pan.)

Into a small bowl, sift together the flour and matcha and set aside.

In a medium bowl, with a handheld mixer on high speed or a very strong arm, beat the eggs with the granulated sugar, salt, and vanilla for about 5 minutes, or until the mixture forms ribbons and roughly doubles in volume. Using a rubber spatula, gradually fold the flour mixture into the egg mixture until incorporated. Drizzle in the melted butter and lemon zest and gently fold into the batter. Cover the bowl with plastic wrap and refrigerate for at least 1 hour or up to 24 hours.

Position one rack in the upper quarter of the oven and another in the center and preheat to 400°F/200°C/gas 6.

Spoon or pipe the batter into the prepared pans, filling each mold about three-quarters full. Bake, staggering the pans so that the top pan isn't directly above the lower one and rotating them back to front and upper to lower halfway through baking, until golden brown around the edges, about 9 minutes.

Immediately turn out the madeleines onto a wire rack and let cool. Dust with powdered sugar and a little bit of matcha, if desired.

kika's coconut

NONSTICK COOKING SPRAY

½ CUP/60 G ALL-PURPOSE FLOUR, PLUS MORE FOR DUSTING THE PANS

½ TSP BAKING POWDER

2 EGGS, AT ROOM TEMPERATURE

¼ TSP SALT

⅓ CUP/65 G COCONUT PALM SUGAR

½ TSP VANILLA OR ALMOND EXTRACT

¼ CUP/60 ML VIRGIN COCONUT OIL, MELTED AND COOLED SLIGHTLY

NAME: *Cristina Arantes*

LOCATION: *San Francisco*

MAD MORSEL: *Cristina, the baking genius behind Kika's Treats, loves these madeleines for more than their addictive flavor. They're made with coconut oil, which has fewer calories than other oils, and coconut palm sugar, which is both tastier and healthier than granulated sugar as well as more environmentally sustainable. Good for the Earth and your taste buds!*

Position one rack in the upper quarter of the oven and another in the center and preheat to 375°F/190°C/gas 5. Liberally coat two metal madeleine pans with nonstick cooking spray and dust with flour, tapping out any excess. Set aside.

Into a small bowl, sift together the flour and baking powder and set aside.

In the bowl of a stand mixer fitted with the whisk attachment, whisk together the eggs and salt on high speed until thick, about 3 minutes. Still whisking, add the sugar in a slow, steady stream and continue for another 2 minutes, or until the mixture is thick and ribbony. Reduce the speed to low and add the vanilla.

Using a rubber spatula, gently fold in the flour mixture just until combined. Fold in half of the coconut oil, just until incorporated, then add the remaining oil and mix just until incorporated. Refrigerate the batter for up to 24 hours or use right away.

Spoon or pipe the batter into the prepared pans, filling each mold about two-thirds full. Bake, staggering the pans so that the top pan is not directly above the lower one and rotating them back to front and upper to lower halfway through baking, until the tops spring back when gently touched, 8 to 10 minutes.

Immediately tap the edge of the pan on the counter and turn out the madeleines onto a wire rack. Let cool before serving.

graham cracker

2 EGGS, AT ROOM
TEMPERATURE

²/3 CUP/130 G SUGAR

³/4 CUP/90 G ALL-PURPOSE
FLOUR, PLUS MORE FOR
DUSTING THE PANS

½ CUP/55 G GRAHAM
CRACKER CRUMBS (MADE
FROM 4 WHOLE CRACKERS)

½ CUP/115 G UNSALTED
BUTTER, MELTED AND
COOLED, PLUS MORE FOR
GREASING THE PANS

NAME: *Lara Starr*
LOCATION: *San Francisco*
MAD MORSEL: *One of Lara's favorite kitchen aromas is the one that wafts
from the bowl when melted butter mixes with graham cracker crumbs to
make a crust for a pie or cheesecake. Heavenly! These madeleines have a
similar scent when baking and a rich, wholesome flavor.*

In a stand mixer fitted with the whisk attachment, whisk together
the eggs and sugar on medium-high speed until smooth and the
sugar has dissolved, about 5 minutes. When the whisk is lifted,
the mixture should ribbon into the bowl. Reduce the speed to
low. Add the flour and the cracker crumbs and whisk just until
combined. Add the melted butter and whisk on medium speed
until incorporated, 2 to 3 minutes. Cover the bowl with plastic
wrap, pressing the wrap directly onto the surface of the batter,
and refrigerate for at least 1 hour or overnight.

Position one rack in the upper quarter of the oven and
another in the center and preheat to 375°F/190°C/gas 5. Grease
two madeleine pans with melted butter and gently dust with
flour, tapping out any excess.

Spoon the batter into the prepared pans, filling each mold
about three-quarters full. Bake, staggering the pans so that the
top pan is not directly above the lower one and rotating them
back to front and upper to lower halfway through baking, until
the edges are brown and a toothpick stuck into the highest
part of the "bump" comes out clean, 10 to 12 minutes.

Immediately turn out the madeleines onto a wire rack and
let cool. Serve warm or at room temperature.

doughnut

3/4 CUP/90 G CAKE FLOUR, PLUS MORE FOR DUSTING THE PAN

1 TSP MACE

1/2 TSP BAKING POWDER

1/2 TSP SALT

3 EGGS, AT ROOM TEMPERATURE

1/2 CUP/100 G SUGAR

1 TSP VANILLA EXTRACT

5 TBSP/70 G UNSALTED BUTTER, MELTED AND COOLED, PLUS MORE FOR GREASING THE PAN

VANILLA GLAZE (PAGE 109)

MAKES 24 MADELEINES

NAME: *Miss Madeleine*

LOCATION: *Boston*

MAD MORSEL: *It took some time for Miss Madeleine to get over the lack of a Parisian café culture in New England, but she soon discovered the gluttonous pleasures of chain coffee shops with their mass-produced dough-nuts. Miss Madeleine concocted this twist on the deep-fried treat. These little cookies taste even better drizzled with Vanilla Glaze.*

Into a small bowl, sift together the cake flour, mace, baking powder, and salt and set aside.

In the bowl of a stand mixer fitted with the whisk attachment, beat together the eggs, sugar, and vanilla on medium-high speed until very light and nearly double in volume, about 5 minutes. Using a rubber spatula, fold the flour mixture and the melted butter into the egg mixture until just combined. Cover the bowl with plastic wrap and refrigerate for at least 1 hour or up to 24 hours.

Position a rack in the center of the oven and preheat to 400°F/ 200°C/gas 6. Grease a madeleine pan with melted butter and dust with flour, tapping out any excess.

Spoon or pipe the batter into the prepared pan, filling each mold about three-quarters full. Bake until the madeleines are puffed up and the edges have just started to brown, 8 to 10 minutes.

Immediately turn out the madeleines onto a wire rack and let cool. Wipe out the pan and let cool. Continue preparing, filling, and baking the pan until all the batter has been used.

When the madeleines are completely cool, dip each one about halfway into the glaze, return to the rack, and let set for about 30 minutes before serving.

vegan coconut milk—
cinnamon

¼ CUP/60 ML CANOLA OIL, PLUS MORE FOR GREASING THE PANS

1 CUP/115 G ALL-PURPOSE FLOUR, PLUS MORE FOR DUSTING THE PANS

¾ CUP/180 ML COCONUT MILK

1½ TSP DISTILLED WHITE VINEGAR

1 TSP BAKING POWDER

¼ TSP BAKING SODA

¼ TSP SALT

½ CUP/120 ML EVAPORATED CANE JUICE

¼ TSP GROUND CINNAMON, PLUS MORE FOR DUSTING

1 TSP VANILLA OR COCONUT EXTRACT

TOASTED COCONUT, FOR GARNISHING (OPTIONAL; PAGE 119)

NAME: *Olivia Fermin*
LOCATION: *San Francisco*
MAD MORSEL: *Olivia loves madeleines so much that she founded Mad 4 Madeleines (which, she admits, doesn't make the most direct use of her master's degree in counseling) and now peddles locally sourced, homemade goodies all over the city, all while dressed up as her favorite Teenage Mutant Ninja Turtle, Raphael.*

Position a rack in the upper quarter of the oven and another in the center and preheat to 330°F/170°C/gas 3. Grease two madeleine pans with canola oil and dust with flour, tapping out any excess. Set aside.

In a small bowl, whisk together the coconut milk and vinegar. Set aside.

In a large bowl, whisk together the flour, baking powder, baking soda, salt, evaporated cane juice, and cinnamon until blended. Add the oil and vanilla to the coconut milk mixture and whisk until blended. Add the wet ingredients to the dry ingredients. Using a large spoon, mix until just combined. Do not overmix. The batter will be slightly lumpy and slightly bubbly.

Using a small ladle, pour the batter into the prepared pans, filling each mold about two-thirds full. Bake, staggering the pans so that the top pan is not directly above the lower one and rotating them back to front and upper to lower halfway through baking, until the edges start to turn brown, about 15 minutes.

Let the madeleines cool in the pans on a wire rack for about 15 minutes. When they are completely cool, turn them out onto the rack. Dust with cinnamon and/or toasted coconut, if desired, and serve.

MAKES **24** MADELEINES

yuletide

3 EGGS

½ CUP/115 G PLUS 2 TBSP
UNSALTED BUTTER

½ CUP/100 G SUGAR

¼ CUP/30 G ALL-PURPOSE
FLOUR

½ CUP/60 G CAKE FLOUR
OR OTHER LOW-PROTEIN
(7% TO 9%) FLOUR

2 TBSP MINCED DRIED
CRANBERRIES TOSSED IN A
SPRINKLING OF CAKE FLOUR

2 TBSP FINELY CHOPPED
PISTACHIOS

NAME: *Lorena Jones*

LOCATION: *San Francisco*

MAD MORSEL: *So much baking happens at Lorena's house during the holidays that there is always a brick or two of butter on the counter coming to room temperature. Sometimes she doesn't have the time to wait for ingredients to come to room temperature, so she keeps a collection of holiday cookie recipes that can be made on the spot with butter and eggs straight out of the refrigerator. This red-and-green–flecked version of her family's favorite madeleine is one of those can-do-anytime recipes.*

Fill a small bowl with warm (but not hot) water. Place the eggs in the water and set aside to warm for 5 minutes.

Meanwhile, in a small heavy saucepan, heat the butter over low heat until completely melted. Set aside to cool.

In the bowl of a stand mixer fitted with the whisk attachment, whisk the eggs on medium speed while adding the sugar in a slow stream, letting the granules run sparingly into the eggs. Increase the speed to medium-high and continue whisking until the mixture triples in volume, turns a glossy pale yellow, and falls off the whisk in 1- to 4-in/2.5- to 10-cm ribbons that sit atop the mixture for a few seconds before melting in, about 5 minutes.

Position one rack in the upper quarter of the oven and another in the center and preheat to 400°F/200°C/gas 6. Generously brush two madeleine pans with 2 tbsp of the melted butter and dust with the all-purpose flour, tapping out any excess.

cont'd

Sift the cake flour over the egg mixture, while gently folding it in with a large rubber spatula. Do not add more than 1 to 2 tbsp flour until the previous addition has been completely incorporated, or you will end up with deposits of flour encased in egg batter.

Pour the remaining ½ cup/115 g melted butter through a strainer into a small mixing bowl. Scoop 1 cup/240 ml of the batter into the bowl of melted butter. Using a small spatula, gently fold the batter into the butter until completely combined. Gently fold the butter mixture into the remaining batter. Gently fold in the cranberries and pistachios.

Spoon or pipe the batter into the prepared pans, filling each mold almost to the top. Bake, staggering the pans so that the top pan is not directly above the lower one and rotating them back to front and upper to lower halfway through baking, until the edges have browned slightly and the center of the madeleines spring back when gently pressed, 10 to 12 minutes.

Let cool in the pans on a wire rack for 3 minutes and then, using a butter knife, gently turn out the madeleines onto the rack and let cool before serving.

GARNISHES

melted coatings

1 CUP/170 G SEMISWEET,
MILK CHOCOLATE, OR
WHITE CHOCOLATE CHIPS;
BUTTERSCOTCH CHIPS;
MINT-FLAVORED CHIPS;
OR PEANUT BUTTER CHIPS

MELTED BUTTER (OPTIONAL)

This is a super-easy method for creating a delicious dunk for your madeleines.

TO MELT ON THE STOVETOP: In a heat-proof bowl over a pan of simmering water, melt the baking chips, stirring occasionally, until smooth.

TO MELT IN THE MICROWAVE: In a microwave-safe bowl, heat the baking chips for 30 seconds. Stir and then return the chips to the microwave for another 30 seconds. Continue heating, checking every 30 seconds, until the chips have melted and are smooth.

If the melted chips are too thick for drizzling, feel free to add a little butter, about 1 tsp at a time, until you reach the consistency you need.

vanilla glaze

1 CUP/100 G POWDERED
SUGAR

½ TSP VANILLA EXTRACT

3 TO 4 TBSP MILK

In a small bowl, whisk together the powdered sugar, vanilla, and 1 tbsp of the milk until smooth. Add more milk, ½ tsp at a time, whisking thoroughly after each addition, until the mixture becomes pourable.

lemon glaze

3/4 CUP/75 G POWDERED SUGAR

1 TBSP FRESHLY SQUEEZED LEMON JUICE

2 TO 3 TBSP WATER

You'll find this basic glaze is particularly good on Bundt cakes and other baked goods.

In a small bowl, whisk together the powdered sugar, lemon juice, and 2 tbsp water until smooth. If the mixture is too thick, add more water, ¼ tsp at a time, whisking thoroughly after each addition. The glaze should come off the spoon in a long, thin stream.

kiera's glaze

1½ CUPS/150 G POWDERED SUGAR

ZEST AND JUICE OF 1 LEMON

½ TSP VANILLA EXTRACT

¼ TSP ALMOND EXTRACT

1 TO 3 TBSP MILK

MAKES ABOUT 2/3 CUP

This glaze is perfect for Kiera's Lemon–Poppy Seed madeleines (page 62), but the lovely balance of lemon juice, vanilla, and almond extract makes this great for a wide variety of cookies.

In a medium bowl, whisk together the powdered sugar, lemon zest and juice, vanilla, almond extract, and 1 tbsp of the milk. If the glaze is too thick, add more milk, 1 tsp at a time, whisking thoroughly after each addition, until you get the consistency you want. (Kiera likes a thin coating, so she uses about 3 tbsp.)

maple glaze

1/3 CUP/35 G POWDERED SUGAR

2 TBSP PURE MAPLE SYRUP

Robyn Goodwin uses this glaze on her Vanilla Walnut madeleines (page 42), but it can also be used on many of the other madeleine recipes. Give it a try!

In a small bowl, whisk together the powdered sugar and maple syrup until smooth.

citrus syrup

½ CUP/100 G SUGAR

¼ CUP/60 ML FRESHLY
SQUEEZED ORANGE JUICE

¼ CUP/60 ML FRESHLY
SQUEEZED LEMON JUICE

MAKES ABOUT
3/4
CUP

This basic syrup calls for orange and lemon juice, but you could also make it using lime juice, Meyer lemon juice, or even grapefruit juice.

In a small saucepan, combine the sugar, orange juice, and lemon juice and heat over medium-high heat until the mixture just begins to boil. Reduce the heat just enough to maintain a simmer and cook, stirring occasionally, until the sugar has dissolved and the mixture begins to thicken, about 5 minutes.

sea-salt caramel

1 CUP/200 G SUGAR

½ CUP/120 ML WATER

½ TSP FLAKY SALT, SUCH AS MALDON

¾ CUP/180 ML HEAVY CREAM, AT ROOM TEMPERATURE

1 TSP VANILLA EXTRACT OR ½ VANILLA BEAN, SEEDS SCRAPED FROM THE POD

MAKES ABOUT 1 CUP

Sarah Billingsley uses this caramel for her Apple-Buckwheat madeleines (page 72). It's good on just about anything sweet or sweet-savory. Drizzle it over ice cream, chocolate desserts, biscuits, or peach pie, or use it as a dip for fruit slices or animal crackers. Although this sauce will thicken in the refrigerator, it's meant to be a filling or a drizzle, so it's runnier than it is chewy.

Measure out all the ingredients and put them on your work surface. You need to work quickly with caramel, so you'll want everything to be accessible.

In a heavy-bottomed saucepan, combine the sugar, water, and salt and heat over medium-high heat until the mixture bubbles and begins to color around the edges. (It's a good idea to wear an oven mitt; this is hot work.) Begin gently swirling the pan. Do not stir! (Stirring makes the sugar seize, or form crystals.) Continue cooking and swirling until the caramel turns an amber color, about 10 minutes.

Immediately remove the pan from the heat and transfer it to a cool, stable work surface. Wearing an oven mitt to protect you from the hot, bubbling caramel (it smarts!), add the cream in a slow stream, stirring the mixture constantly with a wooden or metal spoon. Stir in the vanilla. Allow the mixture to cool to room temperature, stirring occasionally, for about 1 hour. (The caramel will keep, refrigerated, for up to 1 month.)

tomato jam

1½ LBS/680 G ROMA
TOMATOES (ABOUT 6),
FINELY CHOPPED

1 CUP/200 G SUGAR

2 TBSP FRESHLY SQUEEZED
LIME JUICE

1 TBSP FRESHLY PEELED
AND GRATED OR MINCED
GINGER

1 TSP GROUND CUMIN

¼ TSP GROUND CINNAMON

⅛ TSP GROUND CLOVES

1 TSP SALT

RED PEPPER FLAKES

1 SMALL BUNCH BASIL
LEAVES FOR GARNISH
(OPTIONAL)

This jam is the perfect accompaniment to Sean Magrann-Wells's Ricotta madeleine recipe (page 83).

In a heavy-bottomed saucepan, combine the tomatoes, sugar, lime juice, ginger, spices, salt, and red pepper flakes and bring to a simmer over medium heat. Continue to simmer until the mixture develops a jamlike consistency, about 15 minutes.

Cut the basil leaves (if using) into a chiffonade by rolling up 3 to 5 leaves at a time and cutting them crosswise into thin slices. Sprinkle over the tomato jam.

MAKES
1½
CUPS

toasted coconut

**1 CUP/75 G GRATED
UNSWEETENED COCONUT**

Toasted coconut is the perfect enhancement to the Double-Orange madeleines (page 55), but it would also be nice with any of the chocolate-dipped madeleines.

MAKES
1
CUP

Position a rack in the center of the oven and preheat to 350°F/180°C/gas 4.

On a rimmed baking sheet lined with aluminum foil, arrange the coconut in a single layer. Toast the coconut for 3 to 5 minutes, checking frequently to avoid burning and rotating the pan from front to back halfway through. When golden brown, remove the pan from the oven and immediately slide the aluminum foil with the coconut onto a wire rack to cool (otherwise the coconut may continue to cook on the hot baking sheet). Toasted coconut can be stored in a zip-top plastic bag in the refrigerator for about 2 weeks.

toasted
nuts and seeds

Toasting nuts gives them a deeper, more concentrated flavor and a pleasing crunch. Toast first, then crush or chop as needed. Because all ovens are slightly different, use the toasting times below as a guide and check the oven frequently to avoid burning.

	Oven	Stovetop	Microwave
Hazelnuts	8 to 10 minutes	5 to 7 minutes	4 to 8 minutes
Almonds	8 to 10 minutes	5 to 7 minutes	4 to 8 minutes
Walnuts	8 to 10 minutes	5 to 7 minutes	4 to 8 minutes
Pecans	6 to 8 minutes	4 to 6 minutes	3 to 6 minutes
Macadamias	6 to 8 minutes	4 to 6 minutes	3 to 6 minutes
Pumpkin Seeds	4 to 6 minutes	3 to 5 minutes	2 to 5 minutes
Sunflower Seeds	4 to 6 minutes	3 to 5 minutes	2 to 5 minutes
Sesame Seeds	3 to 5 minutes	2 to 3 minutes	1½ to 3 minutes

TO TOAST IN THE OVEN: Position a rack in the center of the oven and preheat to 350°F/180°C/gas 4. On a rimmed baking sheet lined with aluminum foil, arrange the nuts or seeds in a single layer. Using the timing chart as a guide, toast the nuts or seeds, rotating the pan from front to back halfway through. When golden brown and fragrant, remove the pan from the oven and immediately transfer them to a wide, shallow platter to cool.

TO TOAST ON THE STOVETOP: In a medium sauté pan, arrange the nuts or seeds in a single layer and toast over medium-high heat, shaking the pan or stirring frequently, until they begin to brown and become fragrant. Immediately transfer them to a wide, shallow platter to cool.

GARNISHES

121

cont'd

TO TOAST IN THE MICROWAVE: In a wide, shallow, microwave-safe plate or bowl, arrange the nuts or seeds in a single layer. Microwave on high, 30 seconds at a time, until the nuts become fragrant and start to brown.

TO MAKE CRUSHED NUTS

The easiest and fastest way to crush nuts is with a hammer (or any heavy object, such as a rolling pin). Put the toasted nuts into a plastic zip-top bag. Push out as much air as possible and seal the bag. Put the bag on a counter or table, flatten it out as much as possible, and, using a hammer, gently start pounding the nuts.

Alternatively, you can chop nuts in a food processor. Simply put the nuts in the work bowl and pulse a few times until you get the size you need. Do not overprocess, or you'll end up with nut butter!

Just remember to read the recipe carefully. In most cases you should measure the nuts after chopping to be accurate. If you measure whole nuts before chopping, the amount will differ significantly.

SOURCES

AMAZON
Find hundreds of ingredients like buckwheat flour or *pimentón* plus a selection of madeleine pans, including nonstick and silicone. It's a one-stop shop for anything you can't find in your neighborhood grocery, and you won't need to run around to a bunch of different stores. It's also a good source for matcha, spices, and vanilla beans.
WWW.AMAZON.COM

BOB'S RED MILL
This Oregon company sells more than 400 products for baking that range from an impressive line of gluten-free flours to baking mixes, whole grains, and more. Many of its products can be found at grocery chains and gourmet markets like Whole Foods. You can also order from its Web site.
WWW.BOBSREDMILL.COM

KING ARTHUR FLOUR
Headquartered in Vermont, King Arthur offers a wide variety of bakeware, kitchen tools, sugars, decorating elements, and, of course, flour. Its products are found at many grocery stores and can also be ordered online.
WWW.KINGARTHURFLOUR.COM

NUTS ONLINE
In addition to its wide variety of nuts, Nuts Online also sells many hard-to-find baking ingredients, including dried fruit, chocolate, and a great selection of gluten-free products.
WWW.NUTSONLINE.COM

SPECTRUM ORGANICS
This company offers an extensive line of cooking oils, from canola to coconut. Find them in popular grocery store chains and gourmet markets.
WWW.SPECTRUMORGANICS.COM

TEANOBI
Teanobi is a San Francisco specialty tea company that sells matcha powder blended for various uses, including some made specifically for baking.
WWW.TEANOBI.COM

WILLIAMS-SONOMA
A great source for high-quality bakeware, stand mixers, madeleine pans, and any other kitchen tools you might need.
WWW.WILLIAMS-SONOMA.COM

INDEX

C'EST
TOUT!

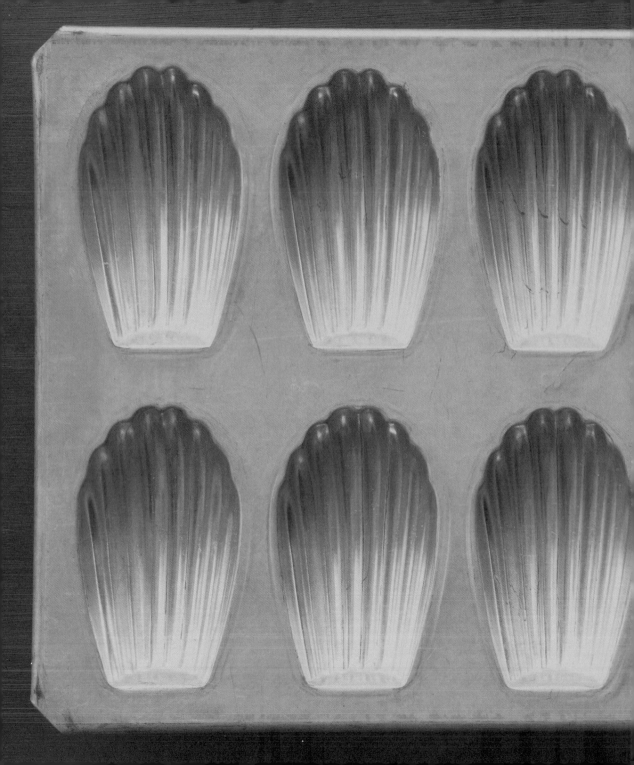